Resource Guide

First Grade Cabin Cruiser

Jokes

Knock, knock. Who's there? This pelican prankster will tickle your funny bone with jokes and riddles. But there might be something fishy going on with that flag!

Dot-to-Dots

Children learn sequencing of their ABCs or 123s as they connect the dots and watch the pictures come to life before their eyes.

Art Studio

Follow this talented toucan to creative fun! Pick from 15 delightful coloring book pages or create your own masterpiece.

Help

Need some help? Don't know how to play a game? The question mark will lend a hand.

Educational Game

Open the hatch and discover an exciting game. Children will get shipshape for school by practicing first grade subjects such as math and English in this underwater adventure.

Movies

Take a sneak peek at what's playing now. Children will want to knock on this door again and again to watch these 8 captivating movies.

Meet Captain Bingham Bear and the rest of his crew! They **can't wait to show off their exciting activities stowed on board this clever craft. Pencil-Pal Software combines educational content with sound, motion, and just the right amount of fun to help first graders be successful in school.**

Educational Goal

This interactive software introduces important first grade skills through a variety of fun activities that appeal to different learning styles.

Educational Content

- Vowel Sounds
- Addition
- Subtraction
- Fractions
- Time and Money
- Spelling
- Letter and Number Sequence
- Rhyming

Developmental Skills

- Following Directions
- Eye-hand Coordination
- Critical Thinking
- Problem Solving
- Listening

Program Features

- Learning is reinforced with audio and animated rewards.
- The simple program design allows children to work independently.
- Drawing, painting, and coloring activities encourage creative learning.
- Jokes and movies keep children motivated.
- Creative themes, adorable characters, and playful melodies appeal to children.

Howdy, Friends!

Write the letter that begins each word.

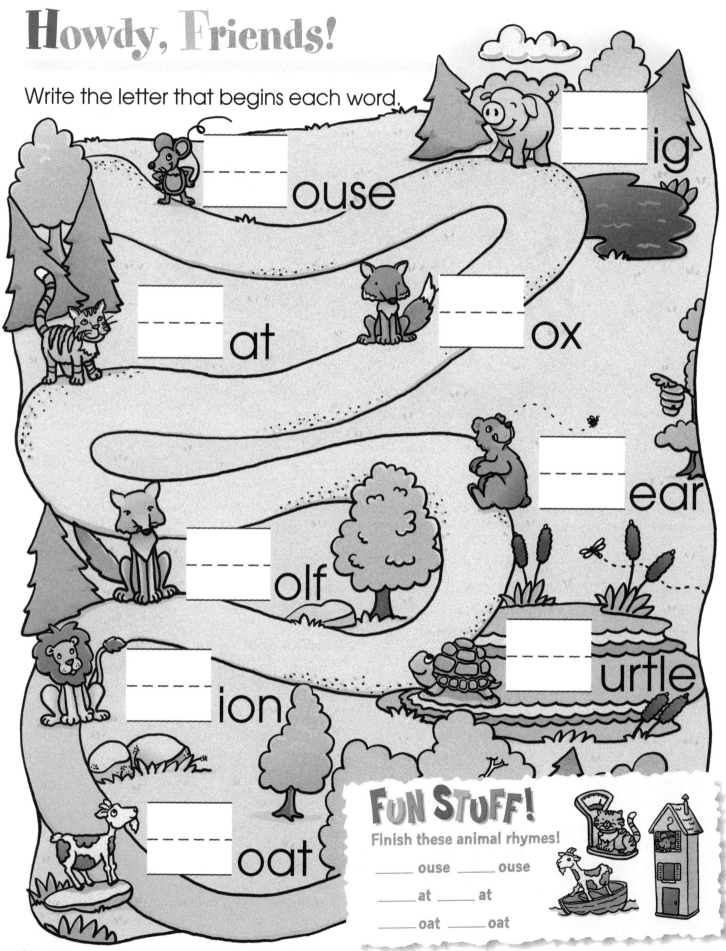

_____ ouse

_____ ig

_____ at

_____ ox

_____ olf

_____ ear

_____ ion

_____ urtle

_____ oat

FUN STUFF!
Finish these animal rhymes!

_____ ouse _____ ouse

_____ at _____ at

_____ oat _____ oat

Birthday Bash Math

Write a number sentence for each picture.

1. _____ + _____ = _____

2. _____ − _____ = _____

3. _____ + _____ = _____

4. _____ + _____ = _____

5. _____ − _____ = _____

COOL IDEA
Draw pictures to go with these number sentences.

$4 + 3 = 7$ $8 − 2 = 6$

Addition and Subtraction   3

Shipshape Garden

This is a **triangle**. △

This is a **rectangle**. ▭

This is a **square**. ◻

Circle the shape for each part of the garden.

1. corn   triangle   rectangle   square

2. carrots   triangle   rectangle   square

3. peas   triangle   rectangle   square

4. radishes   triangle   rectangle   square

5. beans   triangle   rectangle   square

Clothes Patterns

Finish the pattern on each.

COOL IDEA
Design clothes of your own.
Use a colorful pattern.

1.

2.

3.

4.

Playtime Puzzles

The letters **a**, **e**, **i**, **o**, and **u** are vowels.
A long vowel says its own name.

cake   tree   hive   rope   mule

Look at the pictures. Say the words.
Write the missing long vowels in the puzzle.

ACROSS

1.

4.

6.

DOWN

2.

3.

5.

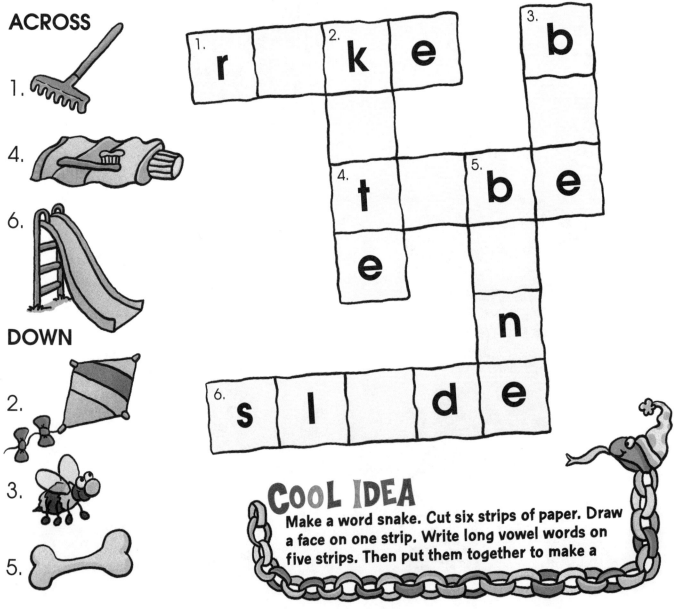

COOL IDEA

Make a word snake. Cut six strips of paper. Draw a face on one strip. Write long vowel words on five strips. Then put them together to make a

A short vowel makes a different sound.

 cat

 bed

 pin

 top

bug

Look at the pictures. Say the words.
Write the missing short vowels in the puzzle.

ACROSS

2.

3.

5.

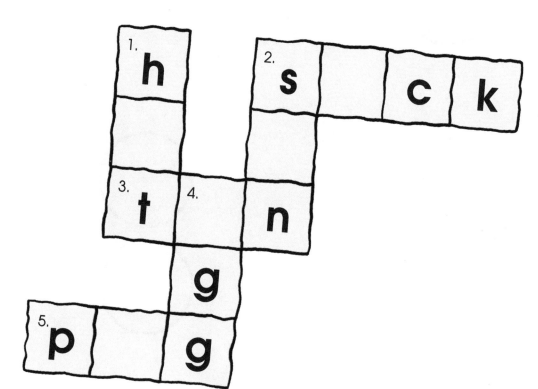

DOWN

1.

2.

4.

FUN STUFF!

You can turn some short vowel words into long vowel words by adding the letter **e**. Try it!

 can + _____ = _____

 pin + _____ = _____

Time Will Tell

Some clocks have two hands. The short hand shows the **hours**. The long hand shows the **minutes**.

3 o'clock
3:00

30 minutes after 3 o'clock
3:30

Write the time for each clock.

1.  _____

2.  _____

3.  _____

4.  _____

Draw a line to match each TV show to the correct clock.

5:00 Cowboy Sam

5:30 Dinosaurs!

7:00 Joke Time

7:30 Camp Talk

On the Job

A **community** is a place where people live and work. Match these workers to the things they use.

FUN STUFF!

Talk to a grown-up about his or her job. What kind of work does the person do? What tools does he or she use?

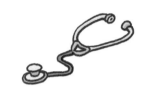

Heart Help

Circle **true** if the sentence is true.

Circle **false** if the sentence is not true.

1. Your heart makes a sound.   true   false

2. Blood carries food to the body.   true   false

3. Your heart beats slower when you run.   true   false

4. Blood helps heal cuts.   true   false

5. Your blood is purple.   true   false

6. Your body is always making new blood.   true   false

DID YOU KNOW?

A grown-up's heart pumps about 5 1/2 quarts of blood every minute. That's more than one gallon of blood!

LUB

DUB

Dino-Myte!

A telling sentence ends with a **period (.)**.
An asking sentence ends with a
question mark (?).

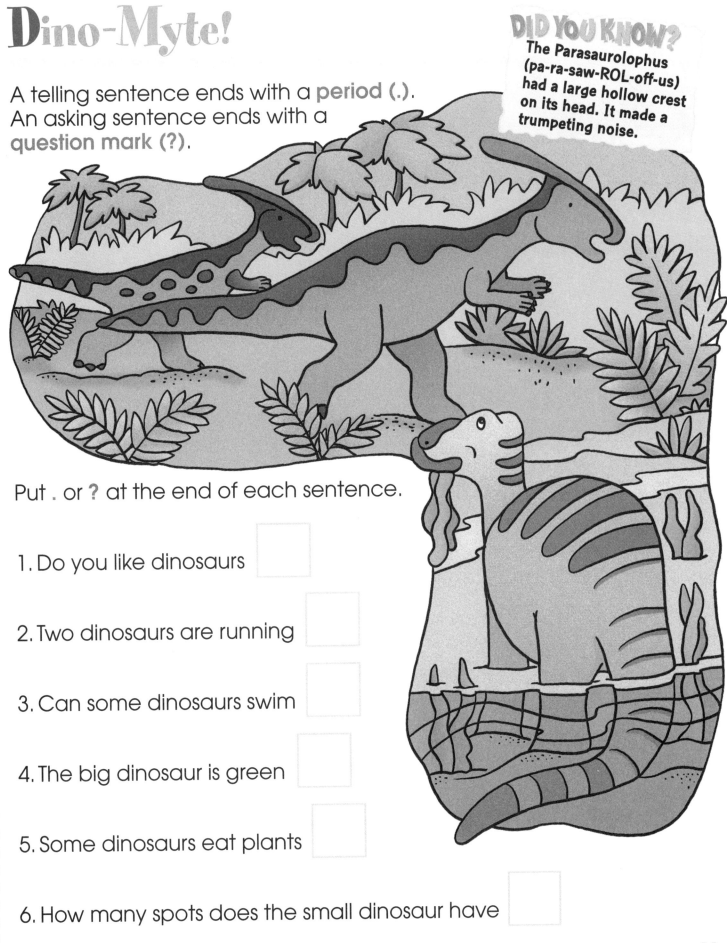

Put **.** or **?** at the end of each sentence.

1. Do you like dinosaurs

2. Two dinosaurs are running

3. Can some dinosaurs swim

4. The big dinosaur is green

5. Some dinosaurs eat plants

6. How many spots does the small dinosaur have

Inching Along

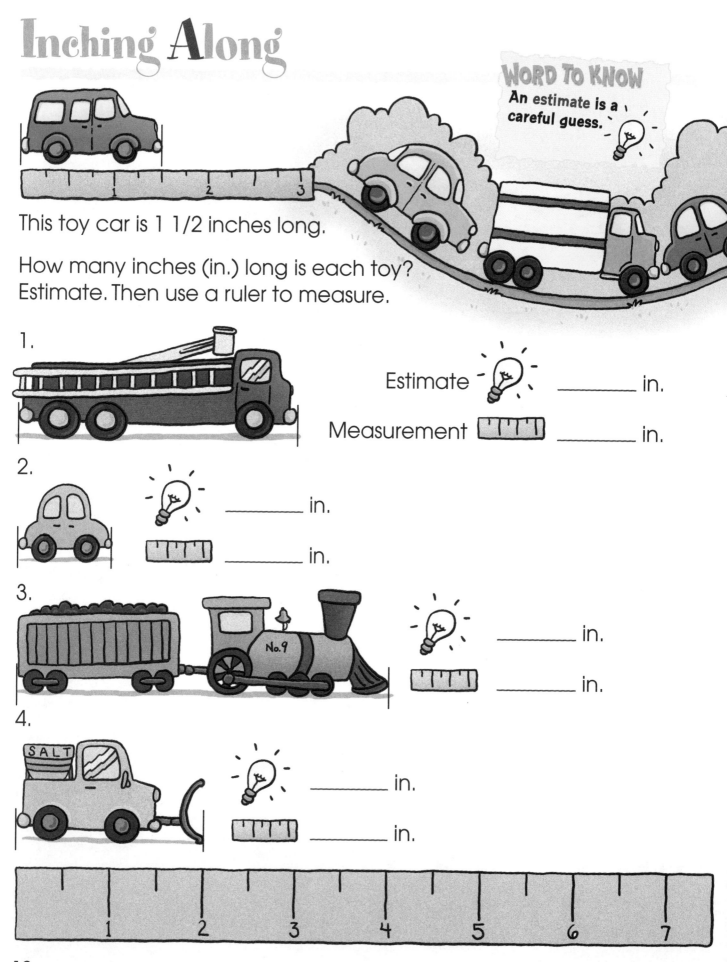

This toy car is 1 1/2 inches long.

How many inches (in.) long is each toy?
Estimate. Then use a ruler to measure.

1.

Estimate _____ in.

Measurement _____ in.

2.

_____ in.

_____ in.

3.

_____ in.

_____ in.

4.

_____ in.

_____ in.

FUN STUFF!

If you do not have a ruler, you can use other tools to measure.

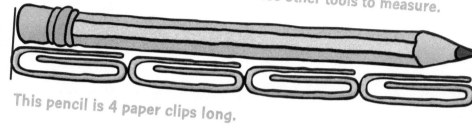

This pencil is 4 paper clips long.

How many centimeters (cm) long is each toy?
Estimate. Then use a ruler to measure.

5.

_____ cm

_____ cm

6.

_____ cm

_____ cm

7.

_____ cm

_____ cm

8.

_____ cm

_____ cm

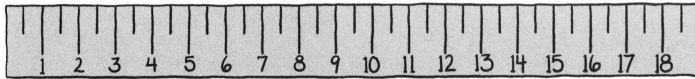

1 2 3 4 5 6 7 8 9 10 11 12 13 14 15 16 17 18

Fur or Feathers?

Most mammals have fur.

Birds have feathers.

Say each animal's name.

Circle ◯ animals that have fur.

Check ✓ animals that have feathers.

Mark ✗ animals that don't have fur or feathers.

rabbit

rooster

turtle

robin

cat

mouse

fish

parrot

puppy

How many have fur? ☐

How many have feathers? ☐

DID YOU KNOW?
Some mammals live in the ocean, such as whales and dolphins. They don't have fur or legs.

Lots of Legs

Most mammals have four legs.

Birds have two legs.

Insects have six legs.

Say each animal's name.

Circle ◯ the number of legs.

horse   0 2 4 6

hen   0 2 4 6

sheep   0 2 4 6

snake   0 2 4 6

pig   0 2 4 6

bee   0 2 4 6

cow   0 2 4 6

ant   0 2 4 6

goose   0 2 4 6

How many have four legs?

How many have six legs?

How many have two legs?

How many have no legs?

All Those Toys

Count each kind of toy.
Then fill in the graph.

| 1 | 2 | 3 | 4 | 5 | 6 |

Off to America

Think about what you know about the Pilgrims.
Then number the boxes in order.

The ship sailed across the sea. It was a long, hard trip.

The Pilgrims got on a big ship. It was called the Mayflower.

It was almost winter. The Pilgrims had to make homes and find food.

At last they saw land. The people were happy.

DID YOU KNOW?

The first Thanksgiving was a Harvest Festival. The Pilgrims wanted to celebrate because they had enough food to make it through their second winter. They also wanted to thank the Native Americans for their help.

Dog Days

Nouns name a person, place, or thing.

sister   house   flower

Most nouns that name more than one end with **s**.

sisters   houses   flowers

Finish each sentence. Choose a word from the bone. Add **s** to make the word mean more than one.

FUN STUFF!

Circle four nouns that name more than one in this pet poem.

Cats are nice, and so are frogs.
But most of all, I like dogs!
Furry, spotted, big and small,
I think dogs are best of all!

tail

bone   cat   pal

dog

1. I have two _____ dogs _____ .

2. They bark at _____ .

3. They wag their _____ .

4. They chew on _____ .

5. They are my _____ .

Pet Search

Special names of people and animals are **proper nouns**. All proper nouns begin with a capital letter.

Find each pet's name in the word search. Then answer each clue with a pet's name.

A	P	E	T	E	R	H	J
F	D	A	X	Z	T	S	P
Q	V	V	G	H	P	L	O
B	U	B	B	L	E	S	L
H	F	X	Y	U	H	V	L
D	U	K	E	W	J	N	Y
A	S	Q	V	T	D	U	Q
D	P	U	F	F	M	K	L

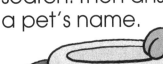

_____

- - - - - - - - - - - - - - - - - -

1. I can talk. _____

- - - - - - - - - - - - - - - - - -

2. I chase mice. _____

- - - - - - - - - - - - - - - - - -

3. I eat carrots. _____

- - - - - - - - - - - - - - - - - -

4. I live in water. _____

- - - - - - - - - - - - - - - - - -

5. I bark at strangers. _____

COOL IDEA

Write the full names of people in your family. Remember to begin each name with a capital letter.

It's Only Natural

Circle ○ things that are **natural**.

Mark ✗ things that are **made by people**.

FUN STUFF!

You can manufacture something from natural things. Pick some dandelions. Tie one dandelion in a knot near the flower head of a second dandelion. Tie the second one in a knot near the flower of a third. Continue until you have the length you want. Tie the last dandelion's stem near the flower of the first.

Buggy Problems

Add to find **how many in all.**

Subtract to find **how many are left.**

Read the problem and finish the picture. Then write a number sentence to show the answer. Use a + or – sign.

1. One bug has 3 spots.
   Another bug has 4 spots.
   How many spots in all?

   _____ _____ = _____

2. There are 4 ants on the log.
   There are 2 ants on the ground.
   How many ants in all?

   _____ _____ = _____

3. There are 6 flies.
   The frog caught 2 flies!
   How many flies are left?

   _____ _____ = _____

Check Your Calendar

The calendar below shows one year.
The top line shows the seasons.
The bottom line shows the months of the year.

Winter

Spring

January   February   March   April   May   June

1. How many months are in a year? _____

2. What month comes after December? _____

3. What month comes before September? _____

COOL IDEA

May is American Bike month. Make a poster that shows safety rules for riding your bike.

Summer

Fall

July   August   September   October   November   December

4. February is in what season? _____

5. May is in what season? _____

6. What month is it now? _____

Find the Friend

A **verb** tells what somebody is doing or what is happening.

The words **hop**, **kick**, and **walk** are verbs.

Roxanne wants to sleep over at Suzie's house. Draw a line to all of the verbs.

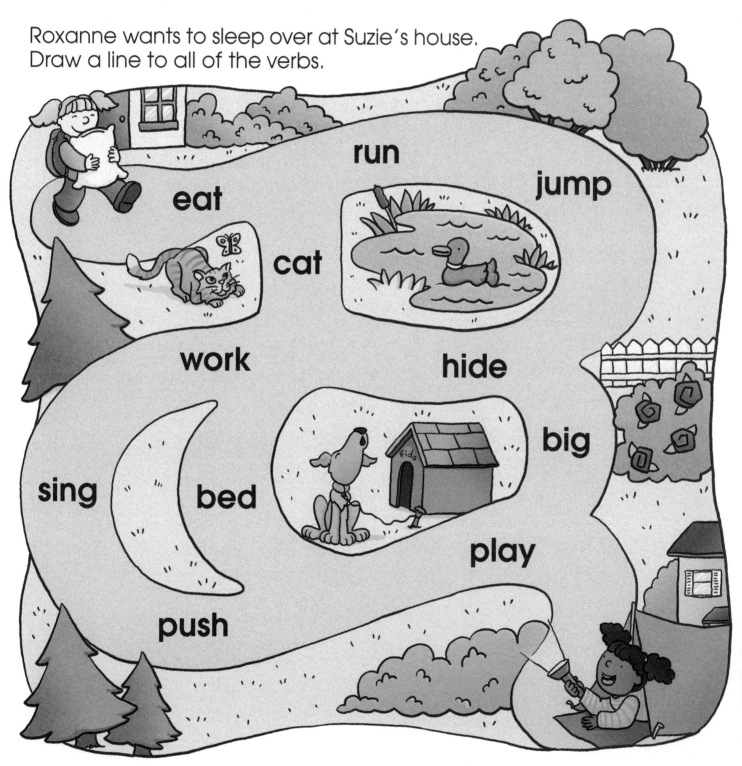

run

eat

jump

cat

work

hide

big

sing

bed

play

push

Animal Map

A **map** shows where you can find things in a place.

Where is the ?

Go across to B.

Go up to 2.

FUN STUFF!

Pretend you're a fly on the ceiling looking down on your bedroom. Draw your room the way you would see it.

Where is each animal? The first one is done for you.

(elephant)	E	5
(tiger)		
(seal)		

(monkey)		
(giraffe)		
(kangaroo)		

Going Together

Write the word that completes each sentence.

hands   little   hear   hot   cave   eat

1. goes with **cold** like goes with _____

2. goes with **drink** like goes with _____

3. goes with **nest** like goes with _____

4. go with **feet** like go with _____

5. goes with **big** like goes with _____

6. goes with **see** like goes with _____

FUN STUFF!

Circle the correct word.

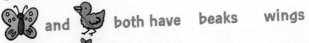 and both have   beaks   wings   spots.

 and both can   jump   swim   sing.

Animal Riddles

Circle ⬭ the correct animal.

1. I have feathers.
   I am white.
   What am I?

2. I have four legs.
   I have a hard shell.
   What am I?

3. I have fur.
   I have a bushy tail.
   What am I?

4. I have four legs.
   I have a short tail.
   What am I?

Who Is the Best?

Add **er** to a word to make it mean more.
Add **est** to a word to make it mean the most.

Write the word that belongs in each sentence.

longest	longer	fast	faster	fastest

1. Tiger's tail is _____ than Rabbit's tail.

2. Monkey's tail is the _____ of all.

3. Mouse was the _____ runner.

4. "Mouse can run very _____ ," said Tiger.

5. Monkey ran _____ than Rabbit.

Toss the Penny

To play **Toss the Penny**, you need 10 pennies and a muffin tin.

Put the muffin tin near a wall. Stand 10 steps away.
Toss a penny. Try to make it go into a hole.
How many pennies can you get into the hole?

Circle the correct answers.

1. Put the muffin tin   near a wall   under a bed.

2. You should stand   5 steps away   10 steps away.

3. You will toss a   dime   penny.

4. Pennies should go   into a hole   in your pocket.

Circle how many pennies you need to play this game.

COOL IDEA

Write a number from 1 to 6 in each cup.
Use the numbers to keep score. When
a penny lands in the cup marked 3, you
earn 3 points. Play with a friend. See
who can be the first to score 10 points.

Food Fractions

The top number of a fraction tells how many parts of the whole are being used. The bottom number tells how many parts make the whole.

Write a fraction for the shaded part.

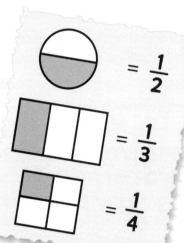

1.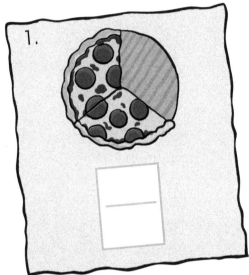

2.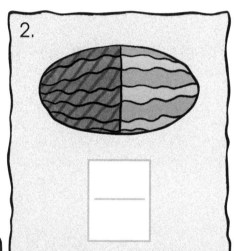

3.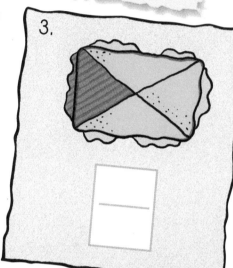

4.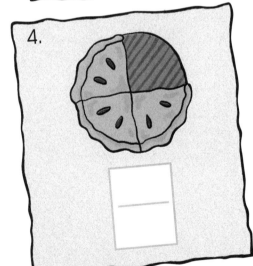

5.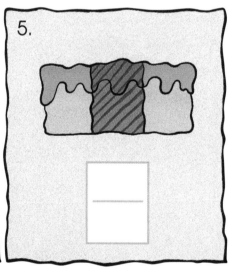

6.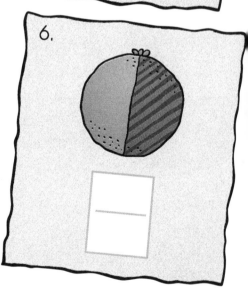

COOL IDEA
Color spaces to show these fractions.

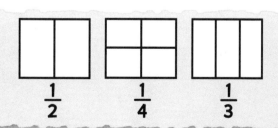

$\frac{1}{2}$ $\frac{1}{4}$ $\frac{1}{3}$

Short a

Say the picture word.
Write the beginning letter to make
short a words.

short **a** sound
apple

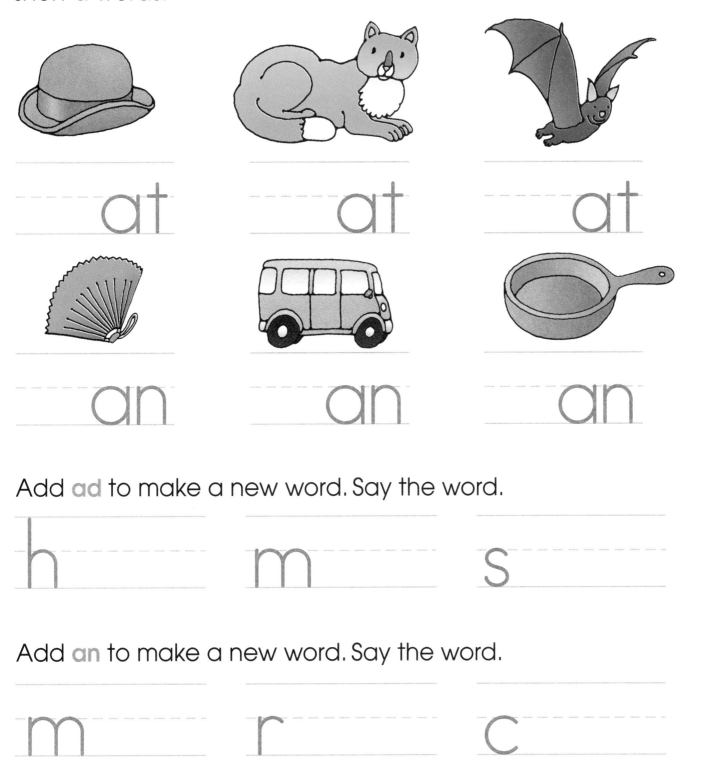

_at   _at   _at

_an   _an   _an

Add **ad** to make a new word. Say the word.

h_   m_   s_

Add **an** to make a new word. Say the word.

m_   r_   c_

Short a

Color the short **a** words **orange**.

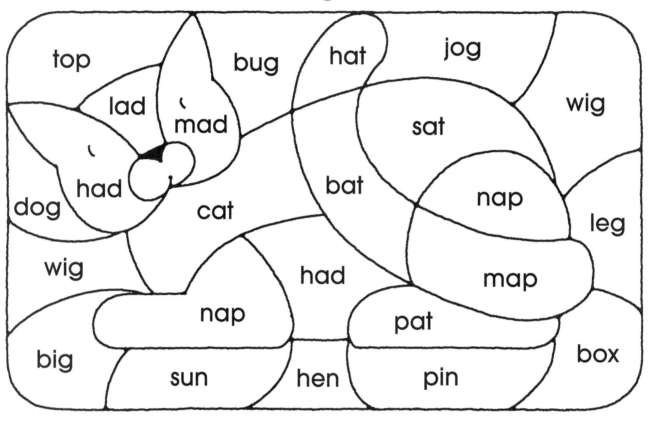

This is a picture of a _____ .

Add **at** to make a new word. Say the word.

s _____   p _____   m _____

Add **ap** to make a new word. Say the word.

n _____   t _____   c _____

Short e

Say the picture word.
Write the short e word.

Short e

Color the short e words blue.

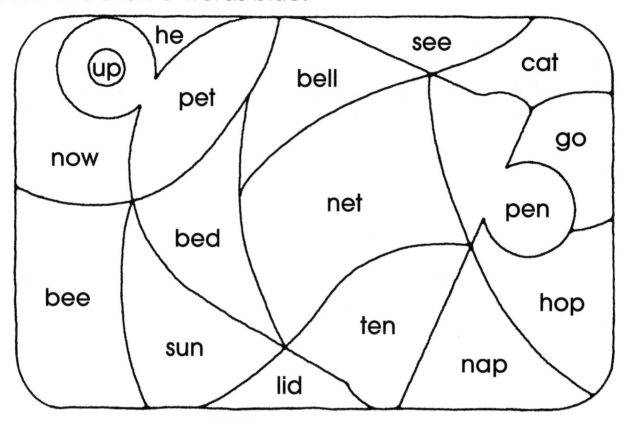

This is a picture of a _____ .

Add **et** to make a new word. Say the word.

g   w   p

Add **en** to make a new word. Say the word.

t   p   h

REVIEW Short a, e

Draw a line from the to the short **a** picture words.

Draw a line from the 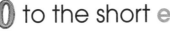 to the short **e** picture words.

Short i

Write the short **i** word that is
the opposite.

| six | give | big | pig | fish | his |

1. little _____

2. take _____

3. hers _____

Write the names of two animals.

4. _____

5. _____

_____

6. The number after five is _____ .

Short i

Color the short **i** words **green**.

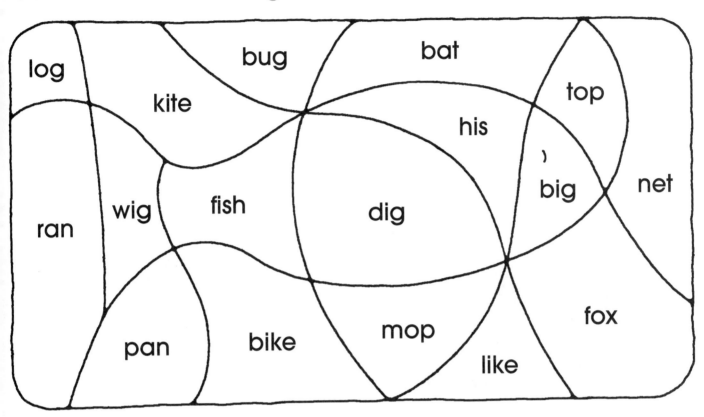

This is a picture of a _____ .

Add **ig** to make a new word. Say the word.

w _____   d _____

Add **ish** to make a new word. Say the word.

d _____   w _____

Short o

Say the picture word.
Write the short o word.

short o sound
octopus

| hot | doll | not | fox | lot | box |

_____

_____

_____

_____

Write the words ending with **ot**.

_____ _____ _____

_____ _____ _____

Write the word that rhymes with **fox**.

_____

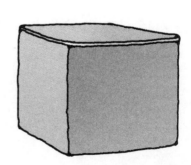

_____

Short o

Color the short o words **purple**.

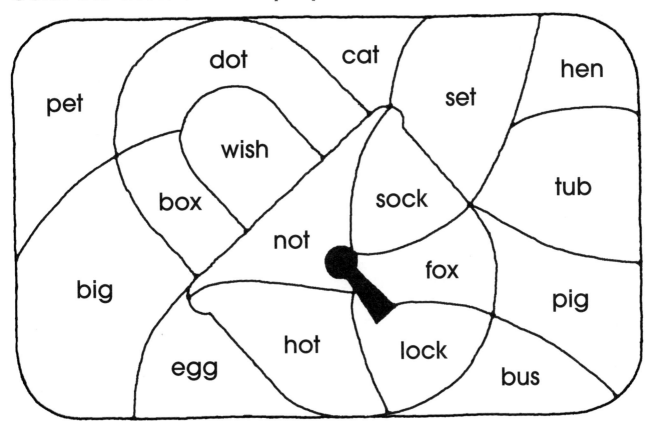

This is a picture of a _____ .

Add **ot** to make a new word. Say the word.

Write two short o words that end with x.

_____   _____

REVIEW Short i, o

Circle **i** if the picture word has a short **i** sound.
Circle **o** if the picture word has a short **o** sound.

Short u

Say the picture word.
Write the short u word.

short u sound
umbrella

bus   cup   bug   sun   rug   hug

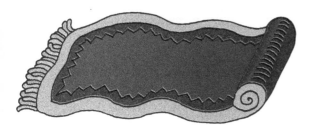

Short *u*

Color the short **u** words yellow.

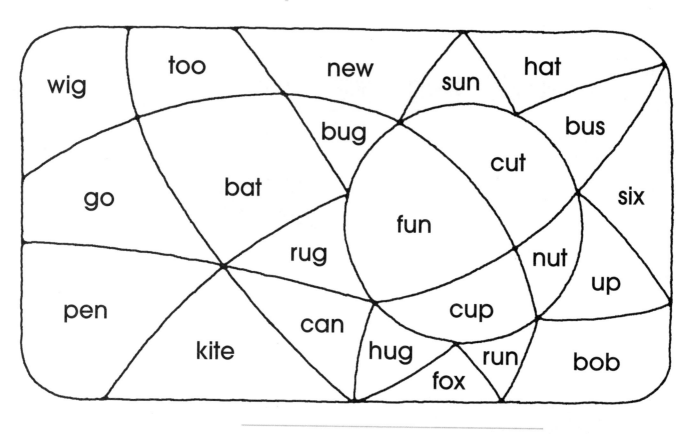

This is a picture of a _____.

Add **ug** to make a new word. Say the word.

r _____ h _____ b _____

Add **ut** to make a new word. Say the word.

h _____ c _____ n _____

REVIEW Short Vowels

Circle the picture with the short vowel sound in each row.

short a

short e

short i

short o

short u

Circle the short vowel sound in each picture word.

a   i   a   e   i   e

Vowel-Consonant-e

Many words with a long vowel sound are spelled with **vowel-consonant-e**.

 c**a**k**e**    k**i**t**e**    r**o**s**e**   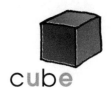 c**u**b**e**

Write the word with each sound. Say the word.
Draw a picture for the word.

| kite   home   tube   rake |

Long a

Long i

Long o

Long u

Vowel-Consonant-e

Write the words to finish the puzzle.

Across

2.

5.

6.

7.

Down

1.

2.

3.

4.

Long a: ai

Write the long **a** word to answer each riddle.

long **a** sound
snail

train   snail   rain   pail   paint   tail

1. J live in a shell. _____

2. J make grow. _____

3. J follow tracks. _____

4. A pig has a short one.

_____

Write two long **a** words that begin with **p**.

_____   _____

Long a: ay

Write the long a word that is the opposite.

| play | stay | may | hay | say | day |

1.  work _____

_____

2. night

_____

3.  go

_____

Write a long a word that begins with the same letter as each picture.

_____ _____ _____

_____ _____ _____

Long a: ay, ai

Help the snail get out of the rain.
Draw a line to the long **a** words.

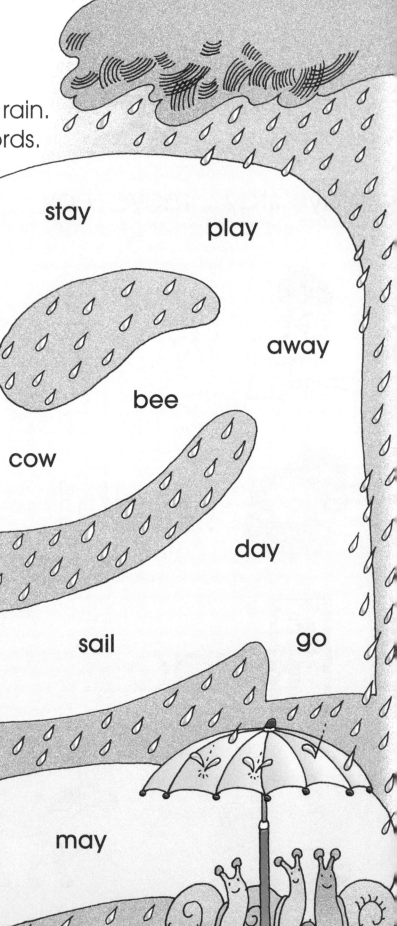

stay

play

rain

say

away

men

bee

train

cow

dog

day

top

sail

go

tray

paint

may

hay

snail

Long e: e, ee, ea

long **e** sound
bee

meet   seal   she   feet   be   leaf

Write the long **e** words spelled **ee**.

_____   _____

_____   _____

Write the words with the long **e**
sound spelled **e**.

_____   _____

_____   _____

Write the long **e** words.

_____   _____

Add **ea** to finish each word.

t ___   m ___   m ___   t ___

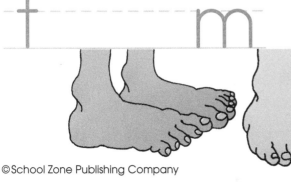

Long e: e, ee, ea

Write the long e word to answer each riddle.

| bee   seal   me   tree   he   leaf |

1. I can swim. _____

2. I am a large plant. _____

3. I grow on trees. _____

4. I get food from 🌸 . _____

Write two 2-letter long e words.

_____   _____

_____   _____

Me? He!

Long i: y, ind, igh

Write the long **i** words that have the same ending.

long **i** sound
kite

cry nine find fly night vine mind right

try

kind

might

fine

Add **ight** to make a new word.

Long i: y, ind, igh

Draw a line through the long **i** words.

fish	find	book
out	fly	his
kid	right	you

pick	pig	night
six	cry	make
mind	this	bat

sky	car	home
not	tight	with
will	see	kind

Long o: o, oa

Write the long o word to answer each riddle.

long o sound
boat

goat   boat   no   coat   so   toad   go

1. I move in water. _____

2. I keep you warm. _____

3. I look like a frog. _____

4. I live on a farm. _____

Write the long o words with two letters.

_____   _____   _____

_____   _____   _____

Long o: ow, old

snow   cold   slow   told   grow   sold   go

Write the long o words spelled ow.

_____   _____   _____

_____   _____   _____

Write the long o words spelled old.

_____   _____   _____

_____   _____   _____

Color the long o words spelled ow **black**.
Color the long o words spelled old yellow.

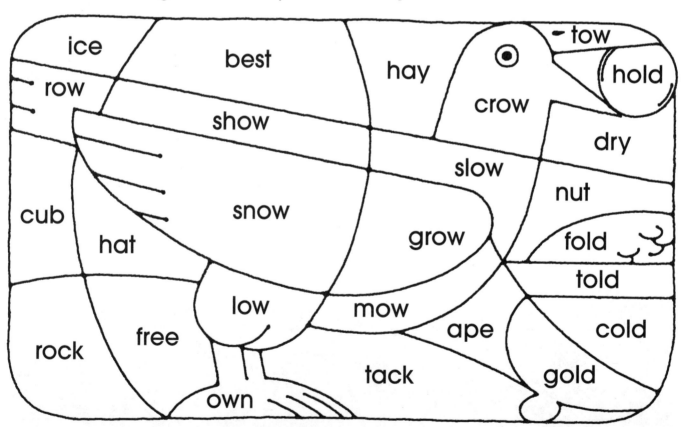

ice   best   hay   tow
row   show   crow   hold
            slow   dry
cub   snow   grow   nut
hat   fold
      low   mow   told
rock   free   ape   cold
            tack   gold
      own

Say the two long o picture words.

Long o: ow, old, oa, o

Help the princess get to the toad.
Draw a line to the long o words.

grow	ring	wake	dog	bell
cold	toad	plum	sled	band
tack	snow	go	goat	took
book	wall	sing	sold	slow
pet	time	bird	chair	told

Vowel Combinations: oo, ew, ue

These words have the vowel sound in .

zoo   blue   new   soon   school   flew

Write two **ew** words.

_____   _____

Write three **oo** words.

_____   _____

_____   _____

_____   _____

Write the word that names a color.

_____

Vowel Combinations: oo, ew, ue

Circle the word that has the same vowel sound
as the first word.

1. **zoo**	blew	run	snow
2. **blue**	boy	food	cup
3. **new**	find	cry	moon
4. **soon**	dew	rose	rain
5. **school**	cold	glue	box
6. **flew**	nest	low	tool

REVIEW Long Vowels

Draw a line from each word to the
long vowel sound.

 kite

 bee

Long a

 snail

Long e

mule

 rose

Long i

cake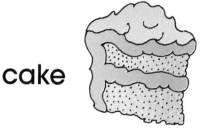

 seal

Long o

fly

 cube

Long u

boat

REVIEW Long Vowels

Read each word. Write the long vowel word that is the opposite.

take	sleep	low	sweet	dry	clean
over	white	go	cold	me	night

1. **dirty** _____

2. **day** _____

3. **hot** _____

4. **wake** _____

5. **sour** _____

6. **you** _____

7. **come** _____

8. **give** _____

9. **black** _____

10. **wet** _____

11. **under** _____

12. **high** _____

REVIEW Long Vowels

Color the picture.
Long a blue
Long e **purple**
Long i **red**
Long o **green**
Long u yellow

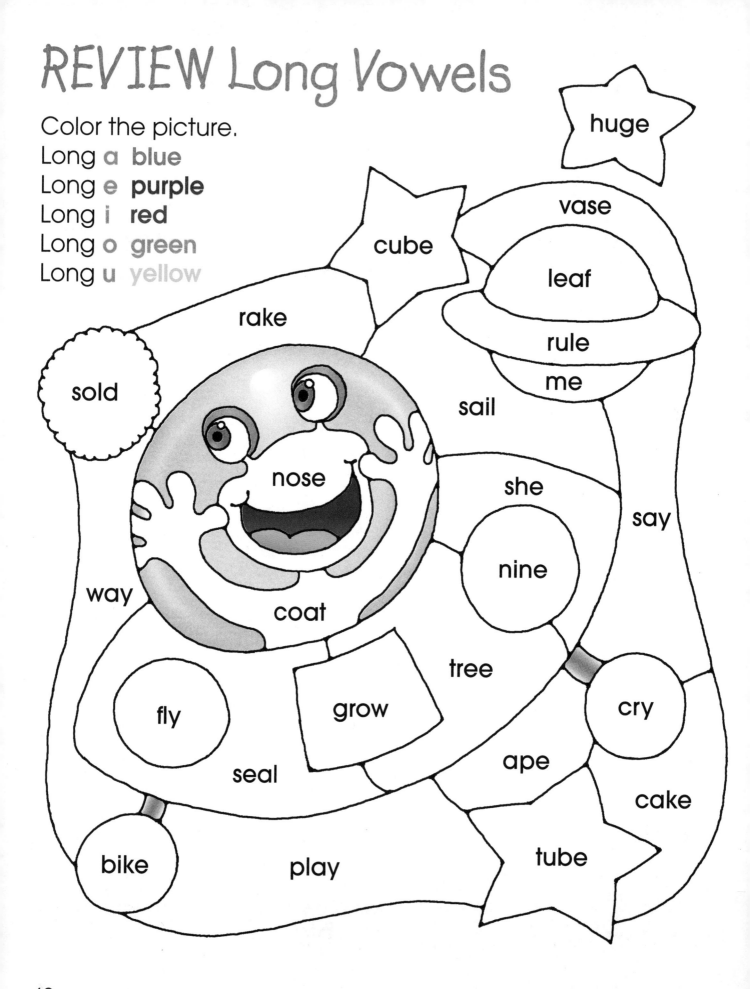

huge

vase

cube

leaf

rake

rule

me

sold

sail

nose

she

say

nine

way

coat

tree

cry

fly

grow

seal

ape

cake

bike

play

tube

Study the alphabet and number chart.

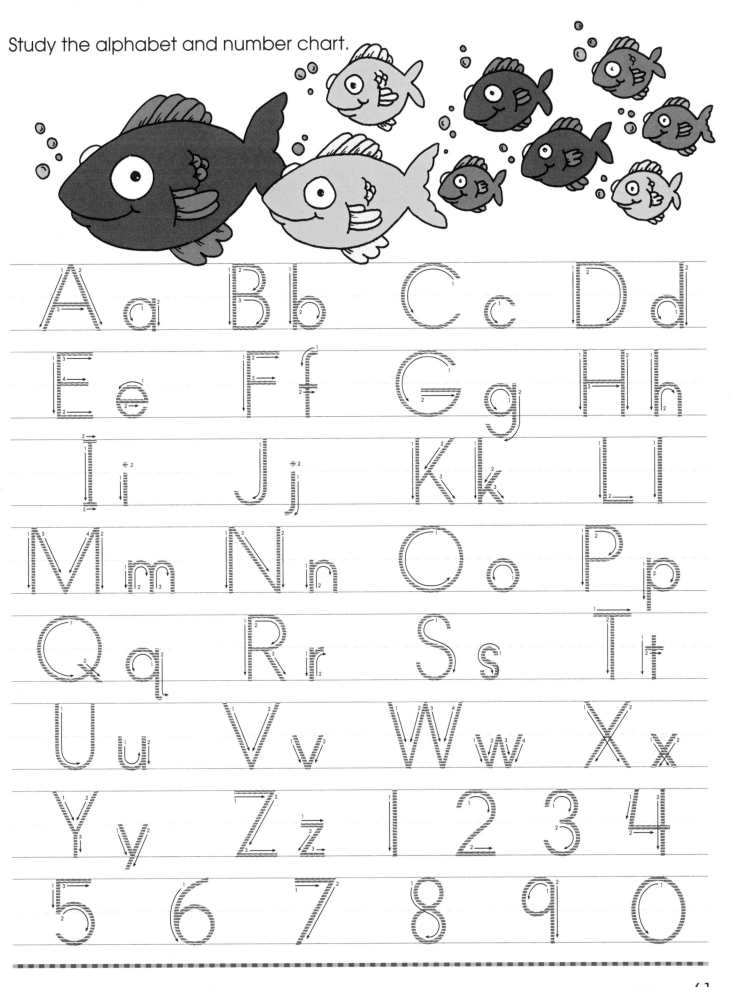

Look at the arrows. Trace the numbers.
Now write the numbers.

1 2 3 4 5

6 7 8 9 0

Look at the arrows. Trace each letter.
Now write the letters and words.

A A

a a

Annie

ant

Look at the arrows. Trace each letter.
Now write the letters and words.

B B

b b

Billy

bear

Look at the arrows. Trace each letter.
Now write the letters and words.

C   C

c   c

Casey

cat

Look at the arrows. Trace each letter.
Now write the letters and words.

D D

d d

David

duck

Look at the arrows. Trace each letter.
Now write the letters and words.

E E

e e

Ellie

elf

Look at the arrows. Trace each letter.
Now write the letters and words.

F F

f f

Fran

fox

Look at the arrows. Trace each letter.
Now write the letters and words.

G G G

g g g

Gary

goat

Look at the arrows. Trace each letter.
Now write the letters and words.

H H

h h

Harry

horse

Look at the arrows. Trace each letter.
Now write the letters and words.

I I

i i

Ike

iguana

Look at the arrows. Trace each letter.
Now write the letters and words.

J J

j j

Jason

jay

Look at the arrows. Trace each letter.
Now write the letters and words.

K K

k k

Kelly

koala

Manuscript Writing 73

Look at the arrows. Trace each letter.
Now write the letters and words.

L L

I I

Leah

lion

Look at the arrows. Trace each letter.
Now write the letters and words.

M M M

m m

Mandy

mouse

Look at the arrows. Trace each letter.
Now write the letters and words.

N N

n n

Nina

newt

Look at the arrows. Trace each letter.
Now write the letters and words.

O O

o o

Omar

owl

Look at the arrows. Trace each letter.
Now write the letters and words.

P P

p p

Peter

panda

Look at the arrows. Trace each letter.
Now write the letters and words.

Q Q Q

q q

Quincy

quail

Look at the arrows. Trace each letter.
Now write the letters and words.

R R

r r

Rich

rabbit

Look at the arrows. Trace each letter.
Now write the letters and words.

S S

S S

Sally

seal

Look at the arrows. Trace each letter.
Now write the letters and words.

T T

t t

Tony

turtle

Look at the arrows. Trace each letter.
Now write the letters and words.

U U

u u

Ursula

unicorn

Look at the arrows. Trace each letter.
Now write the letters and words.

V V V

v v v

Vicky

vulture

Look at the arrows. Trace each letter.
Now write the letters and words.

W W W

W W W

Wendy

wolf

Look at the arrows. Trace each letter.
Now write the letters and words.

X X X

X X X

Xavier

x-ray

Look at the arrows. Trace each letter.
Now write the letters and words.

Y Y

y y

Yancy

yak

Look at the arrows. Trace each letter.
Now write the letters and words.

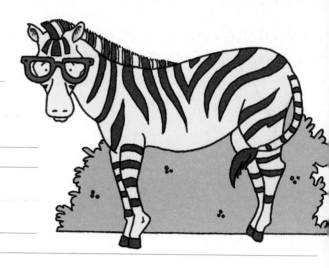

Z Z

z z

Zack

zebra

Practice writing your name.

Wasn't that fun?

Practice writing your address and phone number.

My name is Randy.

Manuscript Writing

Learning to Add

The **+** sign means you should **add**.

 $\underline{\quad 2 \quad} + \underline{\quad 1 \quad} = \underline{\quad 3 \quad}$

The pictures below tell you to **add**. Read the story problem. Write the answer.

1.

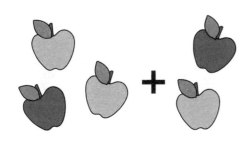 _____ + _____ = _____

How many **in all**? _____

2.

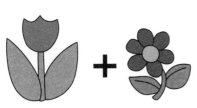 _____ + _____ = _____

How many **altogether**? _____

3.

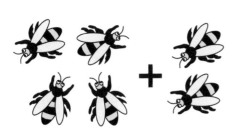 _____ + _____ = _____

What is the **total** number of ? _____

Addition Equations

$$\underline{\quad 2 \quad} + \underline{\quad 2 \quad} = \underline{\quad 4 \quad}$$
in all

Read the story problem. Write the **equation**.

1.

$$\underline{\qquad} + \underline{\qquad} = \underline{\qquad}$$
in all

2.

$$\underline{\qquad} + \underline{\qquad} = \underline{\qquad}$$
in all

3.

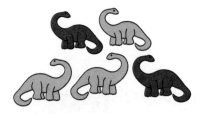 

$$\underline{\qquad} + \underline{\qquad} = \underline{\qquad}$$
in all

Addition Problems

How many 🦇🦇 **in all**? $\underline{\ 2\ } + \underline{\ 4\ } = \underline{\ 6\ }$

Read the story problem. Write the **equation**.

1.

How many 🦇🦇 **in all**?   _____ + _____ = _____

2.

How many 🦇🦇 **in all**?   _____ + _____ = _____

3.

How many 🦇🦇 **in all**?   _____ + _____ = _____

Wet Pets

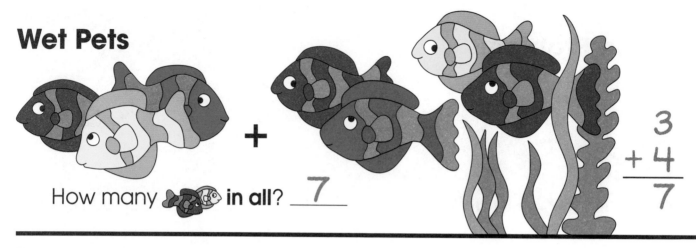

How many **in all**? __7__

$$\begin{array}{r} 3 \\ +4 \\ \hline 7 \end{array}$$

Read the story problem. Write the answer.

1.

How many in all? _____

$$\begin{array}{r} 5 \\ +2 \\ \hline \end{array}$$

2.

How many in all? _____

$$\begin{array}{r} 3 \\ +3 \\ \hline \end{array}$$

3.

How many in all? _____

$$\begin{array}{r} 5 \\ +3 \\ \hline \end{array}$$

4.

How many in all? _____

$$\begin{array}{r} 4 \\ +4 \\ \hline \end{array}$$

Pets

Lisa has **3** fish.
Bill has **4** fish.
How many are there **in all**?

___7___ fish

$$\begin{array}{r} 3 \\ +\,4 \\ \hline 7 \end{array}$$

Read the story problem. Write the **equation**.

1. Hanna has **2** birds.
   Pat has **5** birds.
   How many are there **in all**?

   _____ birds

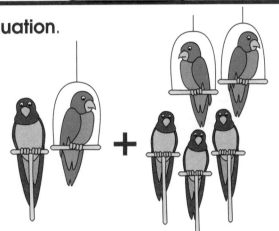

_____
_____
_____

2. Jack saw **3** dogs.
   Then he saw **5** more.
   How many were there **in all**?

   _____ dogs

_____
_____
_____

3. Abby has **2** kittens.
   Scott has **6** kittens.
   How many are there **in all**?

   _____ kittens

_____
_____
_____

Pen Pals

Peter wrote **6** letters.
Tracy wrote **5** letters.
How many were there **in all**?

___11___ letters

$$\begin{array}{r} 6 \\ +\ 5 \\ \hline 11 \end{array}$$

Read the story problem. Write the **equation**.

1. Haley read **4** books.
   Matt read **5** books.
   How many books did
   they read **in all**?

   _____ books

_____

_____

_____

2. Jason has **3** pens.
   Jesse has **6** pens.
   How many pens are
   there **in all**?

   _____ pens

_____

_____

_____

3. Jack has **5** stamps.
   Dan has **5** stamps.
   How many stamps are
   there **in all**?

   _____ stamps

_____

_____

_____

Learning to Subtract

<u>3</u>
in all

<u>1</u>
going away

<u>2</u>
are left

Read the story problem. Write the number sentence. Find the answer.

1.

_____
in all

_____
going away

_____
are left

2.

_____
in all

_____
going away

_____
are left

3.

_____
in all

_____
going away

_____
are left

Subtraction Equations

The **–** sign means you should **subtract**.

$$\underline{7}$$
in all

$$\underline{7} - \underline{3} = \underline{4}$$
in all   **are left**

Read the story problem. Write the **equation**.

1.

$$\underline{}$$
in all

$$\underline{} - \underline{} = \underline{}$$
in all

2.

$$\underline{}$$
in all

$$\underline{} - \underline{} = \underline{}$$
in all

3.

$$\underline{}$$
in all

$$\underline{} - \underline{} = \underline{}$$
in all

Problem Solving

Read the story problem. Write the answer.

1. How many **are left**?

_____ frogs

2. How many **are left**?

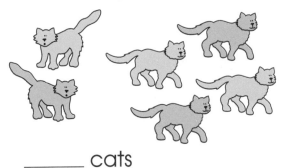

_____ cats

3. How many **are left**?

_____ rabbits

4. How many **are left**?

_____ dogs

5. How many **are left**?

_____ mice

6. How many **are left**?

_____ birds

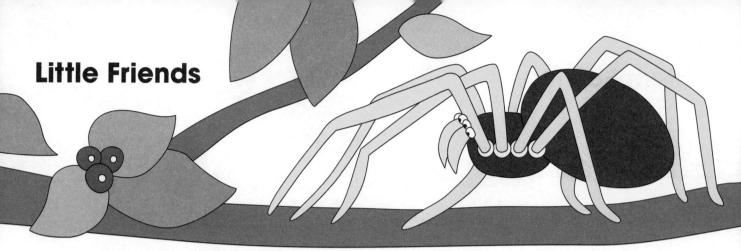

Little Friends

Read the story problem. Write the **equation**.

1.

_____ – _____ = _____

How many **are left**? _____

2.

_____ – _____ = _____

How many **are left**? _____

3.

_____ – _____ = _____

How many **are left**? _____

4.

_____ – _____ = _____

How many **are left**? _____

Bees and Bears

6 bees were on a flower.
3 bees flew away.
How many bees were left?

__3__ bees

$$\begin{array}{r} 6 \\ -\ 3 \\ \hline 3 \end{array}$$

Read the story problem. Write the **equation**.

1. **5** bees were at the hive.
3 bees flew away.
How many bees were left?

_____ bees

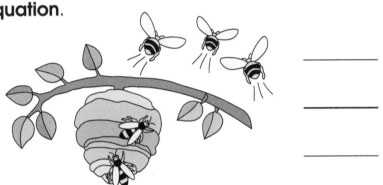

_____
_____
_____

2. **6** bears were in the woods.
4 bears went away.
How many bears were left?

_____ bears

_____
_____
_____

3. Bear had **6** jars of honey.
He gave away **2**.
How many jars of
honey did he have left?

_____ jars

_____
_____
_____

Subtraction Story Problems

Subtraction

Jim had **7** flowers.
He gave away **3** flowers.
How many did he have left?

___4___ flowers

$$\begin{array}{r} 7 \\ -\ 3 \\ \hline 4 \end{array}$$

Read the story problem. Write the **equation**.

1. Tiffany saw **8** birds.
   4 birds flew away.
   How many were left?

   _____ birds

   _____

   _____

   _____

2. Heidi had **6** apples.
   She ate **2** of them.
   How many did she have left?

   _____ apples

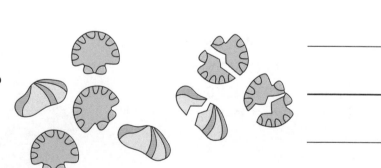

   _____

   _____

   _____

3. Tom found **8** shells.
   He broke **3** of them.
   How many did he have left?

   _____ shells

   _____

   _____

   _____

Add or Subtract

Christy had **7** oranges.
She bought **3** more.
How many does she have in all?

$$\begin{array}{r} 7 \\ +\ 3 \\ \hline 10 \end{array}$$

___10___ oranges

Read the story problem. Write the **equation**.

1. Matt picked **8** apples.
   He ate **2** of them.
   How many does he have left?

   _____ apples

   _____
   _____
   _____

2. Jason has **5** pears.
   Jill has **4** pears.
   How many do they have in all?

   _____ pears

   _____
   _____
   _____

3. Pat had **7** bananas.
   He gave away **4** bananas.
   How many does he have left?

   _____ bananas

   _____
   _____
   _____

Water Friends

8 frogs.
4 alligators.
How many more
frogs are there?

$$\begin{array}{r} 8 \\ -\ 4 \\ \hline 4 \end{array}$$

Read the story problem. Write the **equation**.

1. 6 frogs were singing.
   2 hopped away.
   How many frogs were left?

_____

_____

_____

2. 7 happy alligators.
   3 sad alligators.
   How many more happy alligators?

_____

_____

3. 9 frogs were sitting on a lily pad.
   4 frogs jumped off.
   How many frogs were left?

_____

_____

_____

4. 8 lily pads with frogs.
   4 without frogs.
   How many more lily pads with frogs?

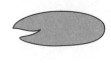

_____

_____

Picture Graphs and Story Problems

SAM

DANA

DOT

TOM

JIM

HEIDI

1. How many baseballs does Sam have? _____

2. How many does Dana have? _____

3. How many does Dot have? _____

4. How many does Tom have? _____

5. How many does Jim have? _____

6. How many does Heidi have? _____

7. How many baseballs do Dot and Dana have altogether?

_____ ☐ _____ = _____

8. Jim has more baseballs than Sam.
   How many more baseballs does Jim have?

_____ ☐ _____ = _____

Picture Graphs and Story Problems

| | CAROL | ANN | NICK | PETE | LISA | DAN |

1. How many pets does Dan have? _____

2. How many pets does Ann have? _____

3. How many pets does Lisa have? _____

4. How many pets does Nick have? _____

5. How many pets do Carol and Pete have in all?

   _____ ☐ _____ = _____

6. Nick has more pets than Dan.
   How many more pets does Nick have?

   _____ ☐ _____ = _____

Bar Graphs and Story Problems

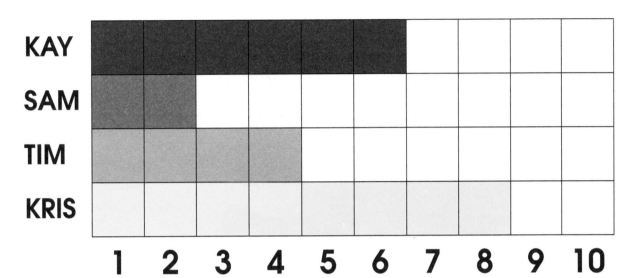

	1	2	3	4	5	6	7	8	9	10
KAY	█	█	█	█	█	█				
SAM	█	█								
TIM	█	█	█	█						
KRIS	█	█	█	█	█	█	█	█		

1. How many boxes of cookies did Kay sell? _____

2. How many boxes of cookies did Tim sell? _____

3. How many boxes of cookies did
   Tim and Sam sell altogether?

   _____ ☐ _____ = _____

4. How many did Kris and Sam sell altogether?

   _____ ☐ _____ = _____

5. Kris sold more boxes than Tim.
   How many more did Kris sell?

   _____ ☐ _____ = _____

6. How many boxes did Tim and Kay sell in all?

   _____ ☐ _____ = _____

Bar Graphs and Story Problems

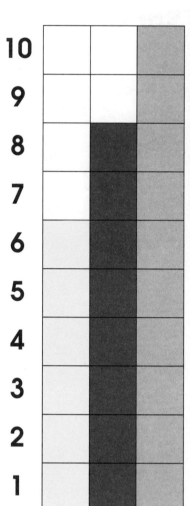

		10
		9
		8
		7
		6
		5
		4
		3
		2
		1

JOE CINDY MIKE

1. How many marbles does Joe have? _____

2. How many does Mike have? _____

3. How many does Cindy have? _____

4. Cindy has more marbles than Joe. How many more does Cindy have?

   _____ ☐ _____ = _____

5. Mike has more marbles than Joe. How many more marbles does Mike have?

   _____ ☐ _____ = _____

6. How many marbles do Joe and Cindy have altogether?

   _____ ☐ _____ = _____

Problem Solving

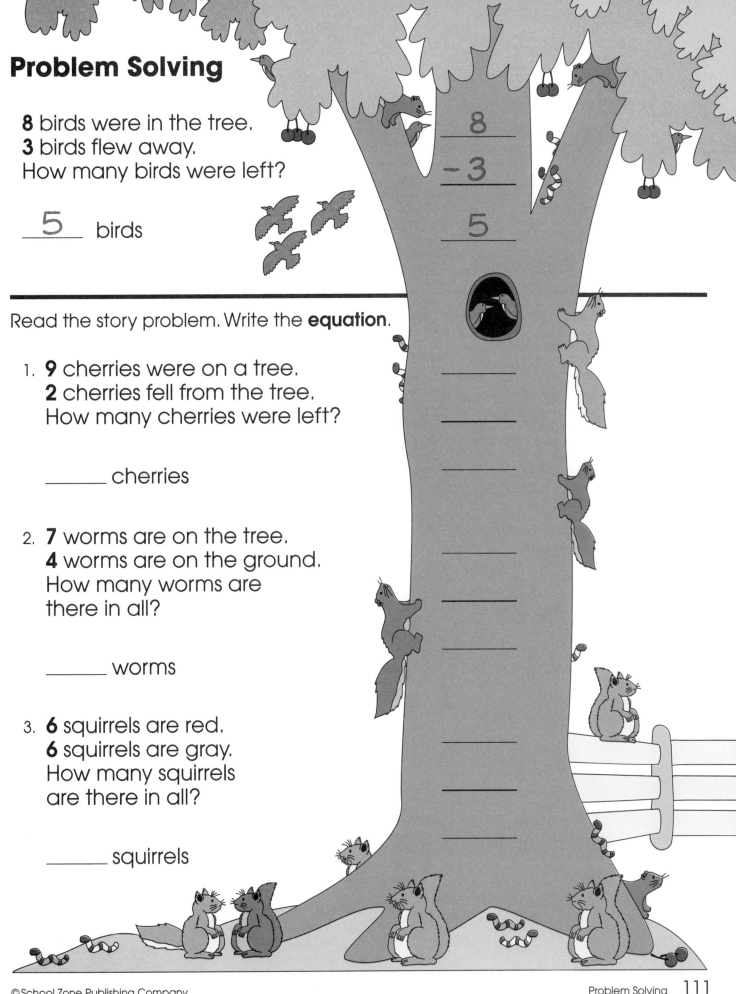

8 birds were in the tree.
3 birds flew away.
How many birds were left?

___5___ birds

$$\begin{array}{r} 8 \\ -3 \\ \hline 5 \end{array}$$

Read the story problem. Write the **equation**.

1. **9** cherries were on a tree.
    2 cherries fell from the tree.
    How many cherries were left?

    _____ cherries

2. **7** worms are on the tree.
    4 worms are on the ground.
    How many worms are
    there in all?

    _____ worms

3. **6** squirrels are red.
    6 squirrels are gray.
    How many squirrels
    are there in all?

    _____ squirrels

Loose Change

David has **5** quarters.
Nora has **5** quarters.
How many quarters
are there in all?

$$\begin{array}{r} 5 \\ + 5 \\ \hline 10 \end{array}$$

___10___ quarters

Read the story problem. Write the **equation**.

1. Alex had **9** pennies.
   He gave **4** away.
   How many pennies
   does he have now?

   _____ pennies

   _____
   _____
   _____

2. Wendy has **4** nickels.
   Jim has **3**. Jon has **6**.
   How many nickels are
   there in all?

   _____ nickels

   _____
   _____
   _____

3. Kate had **9** dimes.
   She spent **3**.
   How many dimes
   does she have left?

   _____ dimes

   _____
   _____
   _____

Let's Have a Party

Deb had **6** party hats.
She found **5** more.
How many does she
have in all?

$$\begin{array}{r} 6 \\ +\ 5 \\ \hline 11 \end{array}$$

___11___ party hats

Read the story problem. Write the **equation**.

1. Randy has **11** presents.
He unwrapped **4** presents.
How many does he have
left to unwrap?

_____ presents

_____

_____

2. Tina had **10** balloons.
She gave away **7** of them.
How many balloons does
she have now?

_____ balloons

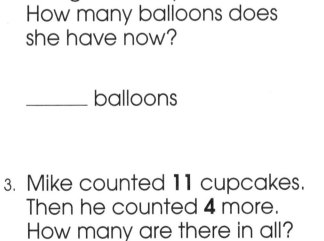

_____

_____

3. Mike counted **11** cupcakes.
Then he counted **4** more.
How many are there in all?

_____ cupcakes

_____

_____

Garden Friends

Write an **equation** for each story problem.

1. There were **10** ladybugs in the garden.
   5 ladybugs left.

_____

_____

_____

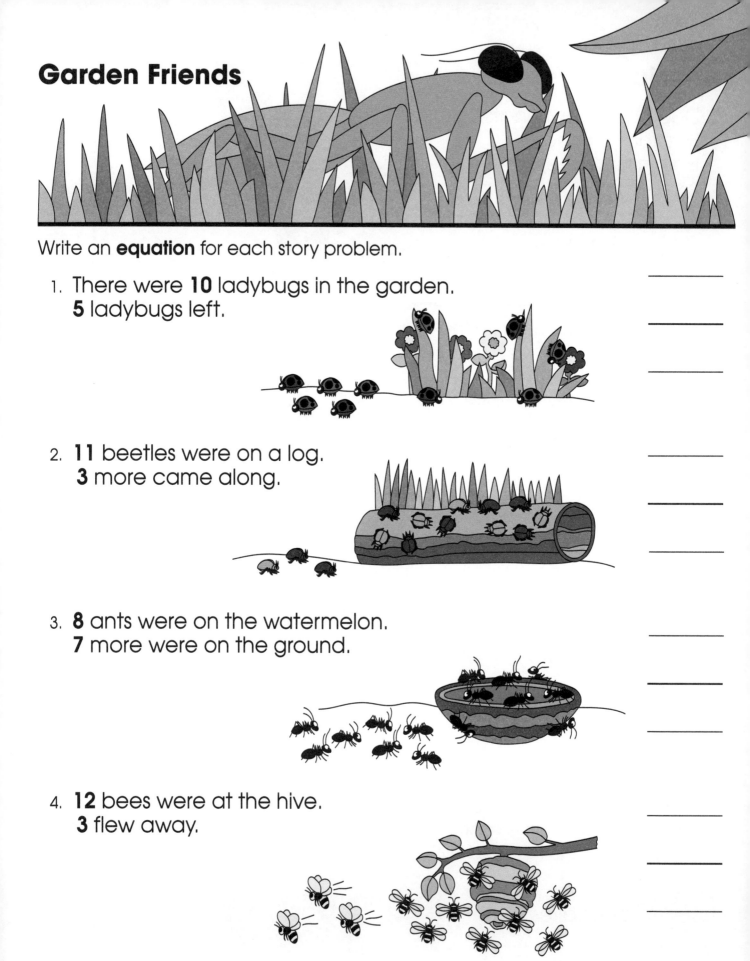

2. **11** beetles were on a log.
   3 more came along.

_____

_____

_____

3. **8** ants were on the watermelon.
   7 more were on the ground.

_____

_____

4. **12** bees were at the hive.
   3 flew away.

_____

_____

Down on the Farm

11 roosters were on a fence.
5 jumped off.
How many roosters were left?

_____6_____ roosters

$$\begin{array}{r} 11 \\ -\ 5 \\ \hline 6 \end{array}$$

Write an **equation** for each story problem.

1. **7** hens were in the pen.
5 hens were in the yard.
How many were there in all?

_____ hens

_____
_____
_____

2. **8** chicks were white.
5 chicks were black.
How many chicks
were there in all?

_____ chicks

_____
_____
_____

3. **12** eggs were in the nest.
4 hatched.
How many eggs were left?

_____ eggs

_____
_____
_____

Summertime

Jerry had **11** cherries.
He ate **3** of them.
How many does he
have now?

$$\begin{array}{r} 11 \\ -\ 3 \\ \hline 8 \end{array}$$

___8___ cherries

Read the story problem. Write the **equation**.

1. Casey bought **14** postcards.
   He mailed **7** of them.
   How many does he
   have now?

   _____ postcards

   _____
   _____
   _____

2. Rita saw **13** sailboats.
   Then she saw **6** more sailboats.
   How many sailboats did
   Rita see in all?

   _____ sailboats

   _____
   _____
   _____

3. Robin caught **15** fish.
   8 fish got away.
   How many does she
   have now?

   _____ fish

   _____
   _____
   _____

At the Beach

Tina saw **7** beach balls.
Then she saw **5** more.
How many beach balls
did Tina see altogether?

<u> 12 </u> beach balls

$$\begin{array}{r} 7 \\ + 5 \\ \hline 12 \end{array}$$

Read the story problem. Write the **equation**.

1. Brian had **16** fishhooks.
   He lost **4** of them.
   How many fishhooks
   does he have left?

   _____ fishhooks

   _____
   _____
   _____

2. Mandy took **13** pictures.
   Then she took **5** more pictures.
   How many did she take in all?

   _____ pictures

   _____
   _____
   _____

3. Jan found **12** shells.
   7 shells broke.
   How many shells does
   she have left?

   _____ shells

   _____
   _____
   _____

Adding and Subtracting

Signs of Spring

Barry saw **16** ladybugs.
8 flew away.
How many were left?

___8___ ladybugs

$$\begin{array}{r} 16 \\ -8 \\ \hline 8 \end{array}$$

Read the story problem. Write the **equation**.

1. Maggie saw **13** tulips at school.
   She saw **11** more at home.
   How many did she see in all?

   _____ tulips

   _____
   _____
   _____

2. Haley had **23** plants.
   She bought **14** more plants.
   How many were there in all?

   _____ plants

   _____
   _____
   _____

3. Luis saw **34** butterflies.
   13 flew away.
   How many were left?

   _____ butterflies

   _____
   _____
   _____

4. Karla had **25¢**.
   She spent **15¢** for seeds.
   How much did she have left?

   _____ ¢

   _____ ¢
   _____ ¢
   _____ ¢

Springtime Fun

= 1¢ = 5¢ = 10¢

5¢ 4¢ 8¢ 6¢ 3¢

Look at the pictures. Solve the problem.

1. Lisa bought a

and a

$$\begin{array}{r} 8¢ \\ +\ 4¢ \\ \hline 12¢ \end{array}$$

What is the sum? 12¢

2. Jerry bought a _____ ¢

and a _____ ¢

and a _____ ¢

What is the total? _____ ¢

3. Mark had

_____ ¢

He bought a _____ ¢

How much is left? _____ ¢

4. Jenny had

_____ ¢

She bought a _____ ¢

How much is left? _____ ¢

At the Ballpark

6¢   5¢   8¢   3¢   7¢   11¢   9¢

Read the story problem. Write the **equation**.

1. Jackie had **48¢**

She bought a

How much did she have left?

$$48¢$$
$$- \ 6¢$$
$$42¢$$

2. Jim bought a

and a

How much did he spend?

_____

_____

_____

3. Jan bought

and a

How much did she spend?

_____

_____

_____

4. Marcie had **15¢**

She bought a

How much did she have left?

_____

_____

_____

5. Ted bought a

and a

How much did he spend?

_____

_____

_____

6. Rich had **12¢**

He bought

How much did he have left?

_____

_____

_____

Hobbies

Read the story problem. Write the **equation**.

1. Haley collects old coins.
   She has **37** old nickels and
   43 old pennies. How many more
   pennies than nickels does she have?

   _____

   _____

2. Peter collects stamps.
   He has **29** United States stamps.
   34 stamps are from other countries.
   How many stamps does he
   have in all?

   _____

   _____

3. Hanna collects buttons.
   She has **58** in her collection.
   Her aunt sent her **18** more.
   How many buttons does she
   have altogether?

   _____

   _____

4. Juan and Maria collect wildflowers.
   Juan has **38** in his collection.
   Maria has **56**. How many more
   wildflowers does Maria
   have than Juan?

   _____

   _____

Solving Story Problems

Read the story problem. Write the **equation**.

1. **129** children attend Hawthorn
   School. **148** attend Henry School.
   How many more children go
   to Henry School?

   _____

   _____

   _____

2. There were **138** adults at the game.
   There were **126** children.
   How many people were at the
   game altogether?

   _____

   _____

3. The Jays scored **79** points during
   the game. The Tigers scored **87**.
   How many more points did the
   Tigers score?

   _____

   _____

   _____

4. **116** hot dogs with mustard were sold.
   118 hot dogs with ketchup were sold.
   How many hot dogs were
   sold altogether?

   _____

   _____

Pennies, Nickels and Dimes

Penny

When we count **pennies** we count by **ones**.

Nickel

When we count **nickels** we count by **fives**.

Dime

When we count **dimes** we count by **tens**.

Write the amount on the line.

1. _____ 7 ¢

2. _____ ¢

It makes sense to count your cents!

3. _____ ¢

4. _____ ¢

Can You Count These Coins?

What is the price of each toy?
Count the coins below. Write the amounts on the lines.

28¢

<u>10</u> <u>20</u> <u>25</u> <u>26</u> <u>27</u> <u>28</u>

1.

     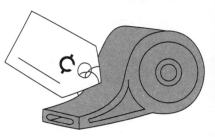

_____

2.

_____

3.

_____

4.

_____

Counting Pennies, Nickels, and Dimes

Count the coins in each group.
Write the amount on the line.

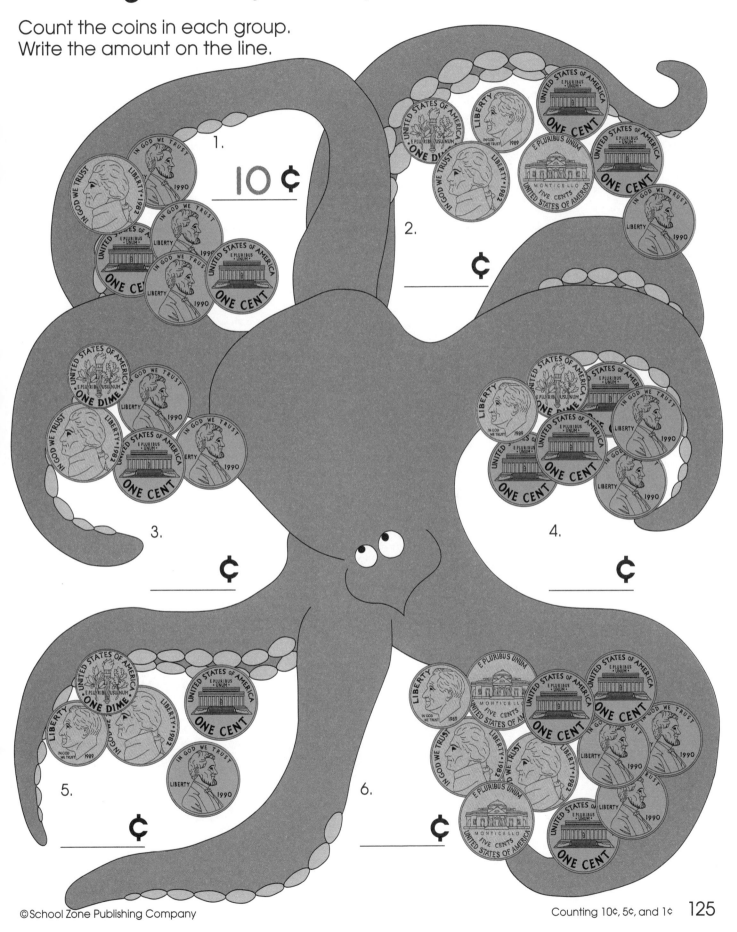

1. __10__ ¢

2. _____ ¢

3. _____ ¢

4. _____ ¢

5. _____ ¢

6. _____ ¢

How Much Money Is a Quarter?

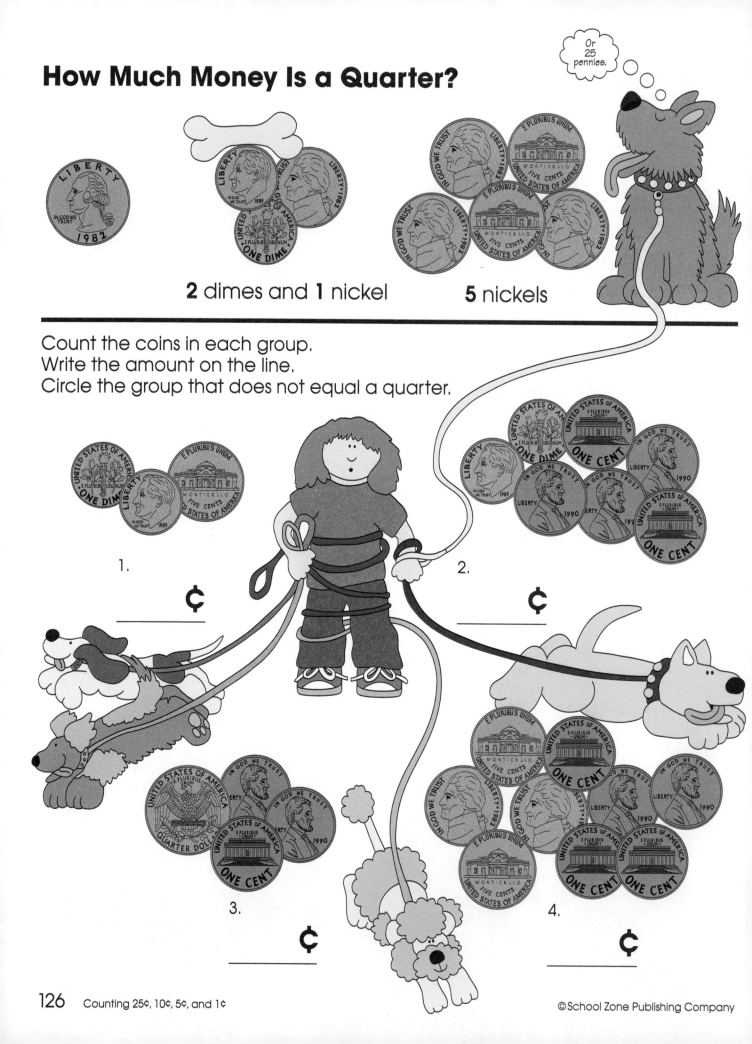

Or 25 pennies.

2 dimes and **1** nickel   **5** nickels

Count the coins in each group.
Write the amount on the line.
Circle the group that does not equal a quarter.

1. _____ ¢

2. _____ ¢

3. _____ ¢

4. _____ ¢

More Quarters

25¢   50¢   75¢

How much do these cost? Write the amount on the line.

1. 36¢

2. _____ ¢

3. _____ ¢

4. _____ ¢

5. _____ ¢

Is There Enough?

Write the amounts on the lines. Is there enough money to pay for this?

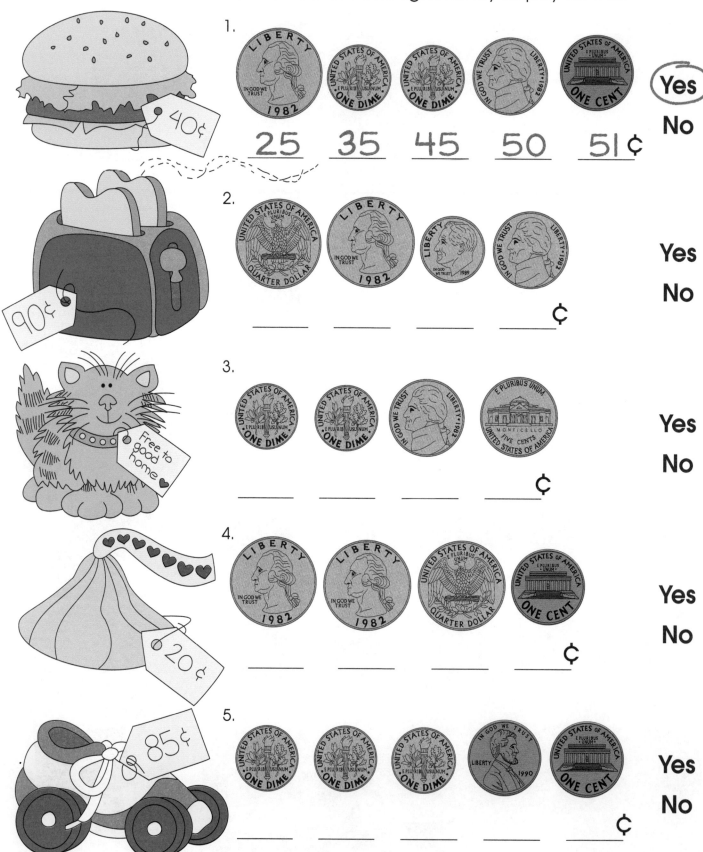

1. 25   35   45   50   51 ¢   **Yes** **No**

2. ___ ___ ___ ___ ¢   **Yes** **No**

3. ___ ___ ___ ___ ¢   **Yes** **No**

4. ___ ___ ___ ___ ¢   **Yes** **No**

5. ___ ___ ___ ___ ¢   **Yes** **No**

How Much Is a Half Dollar?

Or 50 pennies.

2 quarters   **5** dimes   **10** nickels

Fill in the number of coins needed to make the correct amount.

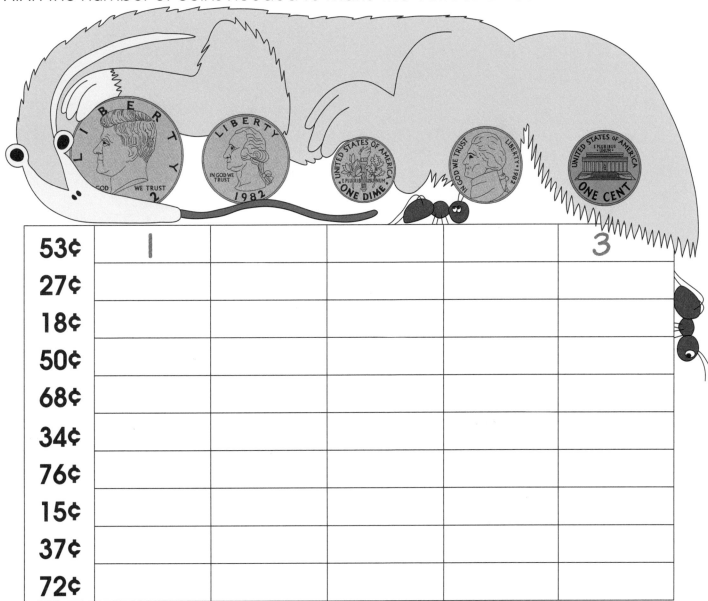

53¢	1				3
27¢					
18¢					
50¢					
68¢					
34¢					
76¢					
15¢					
37¢					
72¢					

Which Coins Total a Half Dollar?

Count the money in each bank.
Circle the coins on the banks that have the exact change for a half dollar.

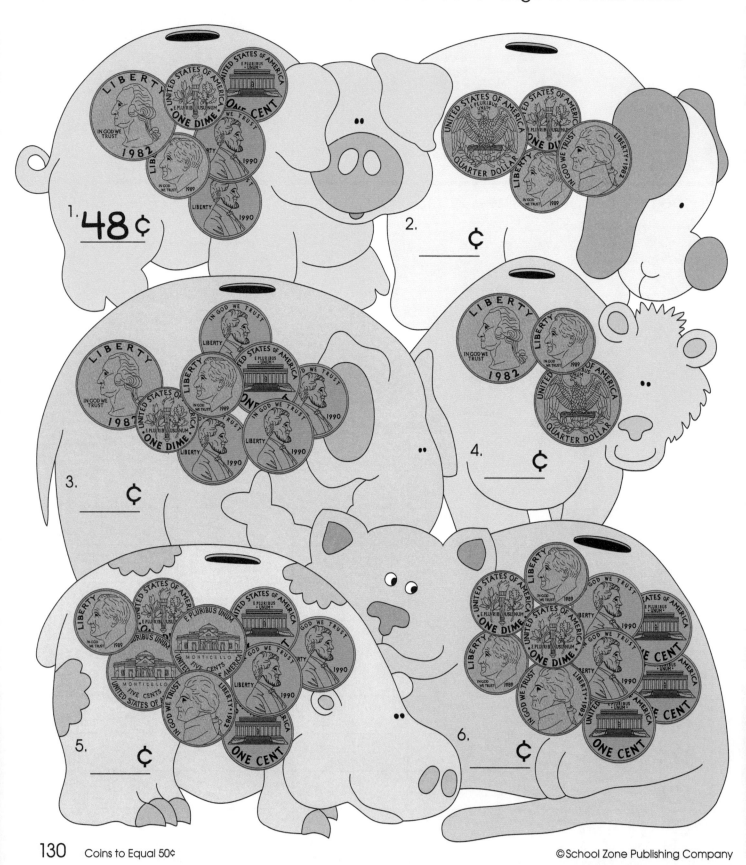

1. 48¢

2. ____ ¢

3. ____ ¢

4. ____ ¢

5. ____ ¢

6. ____ ¢

Going to the Store

How much does each item cost?
How much does it cost in all?

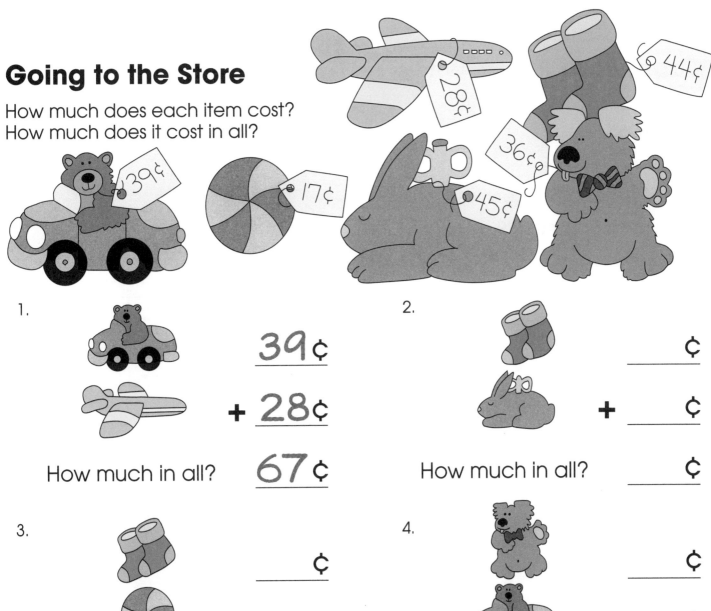

1.

$$\underline{39}¢$$
$$+\ \underline{28}¢$$

How much in all? $\underline{67}¢$

2.

_____ ¢
$+$ _____ ¢

How much in all?   _____ ¢

3.

_____ ¢
$+$ _____ ¢

How much in all?   _____ ¢

4.

_____ ¢
$+$ _____ ¢

How much in all?   _____ ¢

5.

_____ ¢
$+$ _____ ¢

How much in all?   _____ ¢

6.

_____ ¢
$+$ _____ ¢

How much in all?   _____ ¢

Crossword Puzzle with Numbers

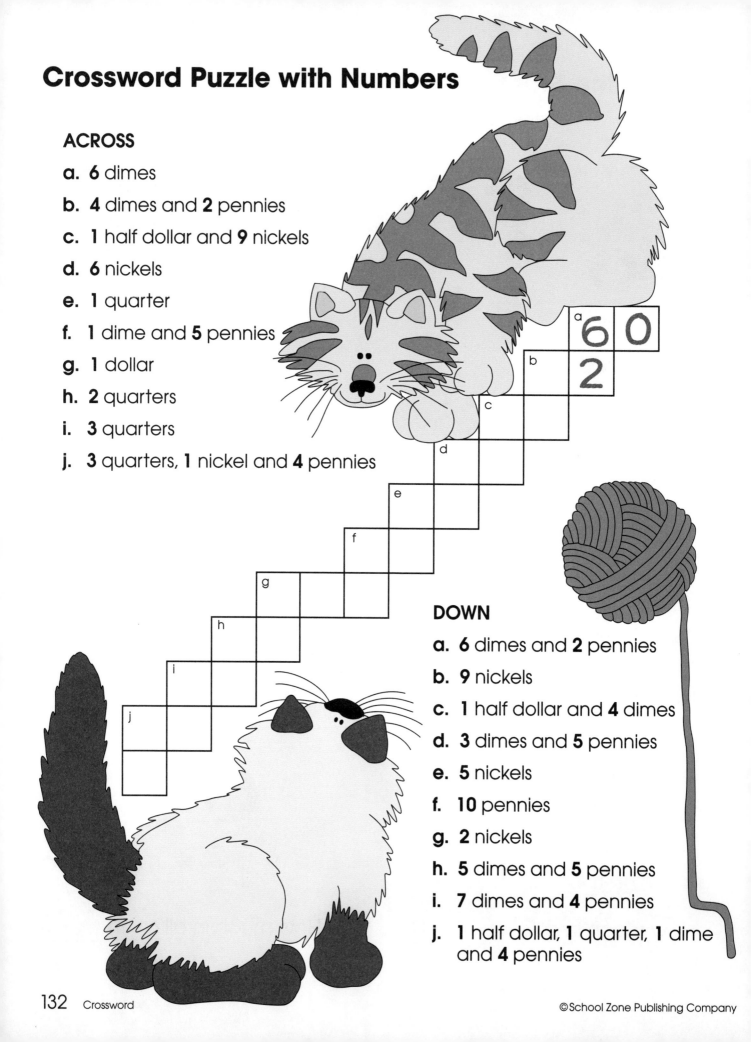

ACROSS

a. **6** dimes

b. **4** dimes and **2** pennies

c. **1** half dollar and **9** nickels

d. **6** nickels

e. **1** quarter

f. **1** dime and **5** pennies

g. **1** dollar

h. **2** quarters

i. **3** quarters

j. **3** quarters, **1** nickel and **4** pennies

DOWN

a. **6** dimes and **2** pennies

b. **9** nickels

c. **1** half dollar and **4** dimes

d. **3** dimes and **5** pennies

e. **5** nickels

f. **10** pennies

g. **2** nickels

h. **5** dimes and **5** pennies

i. **7** dimes and **4** pennies

j. **1** half dollar, **1** quarter, **1** dime and **4** pennies

Same Size, Same Shape

Look at the shapes. Each shape has two parts.
Each part is the same size and same shape.

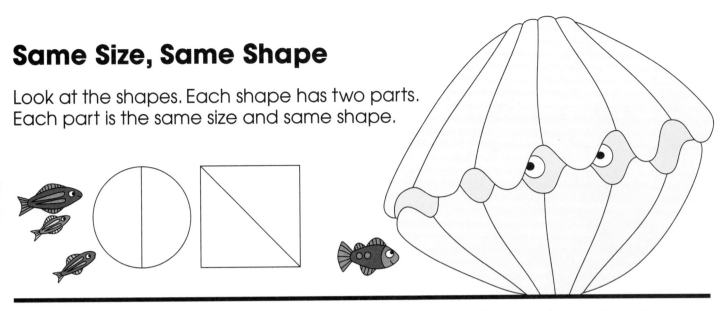

Circle the objects below that have the **same size** and **same shaped** parts.

1.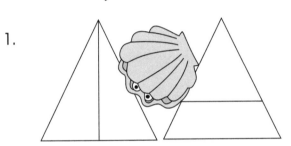

2.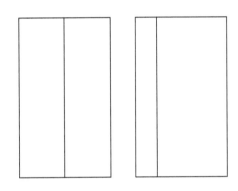

3.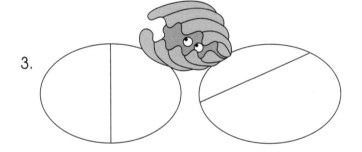

4.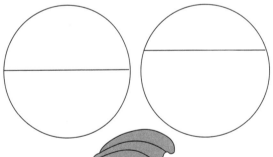

5.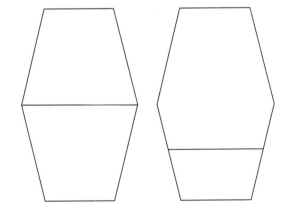

6.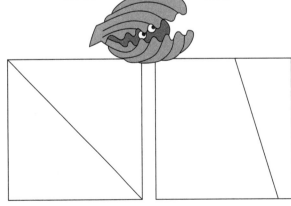

Parts of an object that are the **same size** and **same shape** are **congruent parts**.

Equal Parts

Look at the shapes. Each shape has two equal parts.
Each part is $\frac{1}{2}$ or **one half**.

 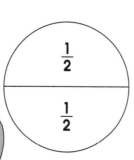 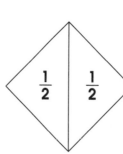 

Write the fraction $\frac{1}{2}$ in each part.

1.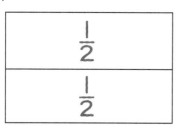

2.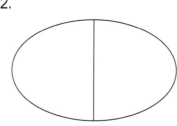

3.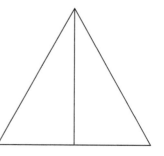

4.

Color $\frac{1}{2}$ of each shape. The first one is done for you.

5.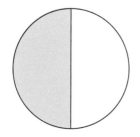

6.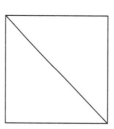

7.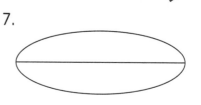

8.

9.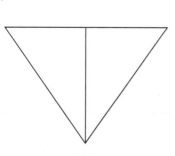

10.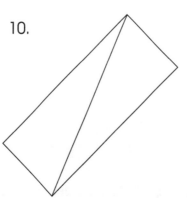

11.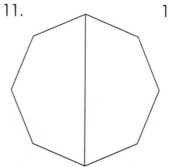

12.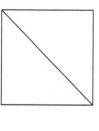

Same Size, Same Shape

Look at the shapes. Each shape has **4** equal parts. Each part is the same size and shape.

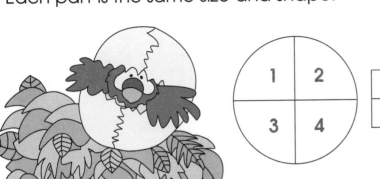

Color the objects below that have the same size and same shaped parts.

1.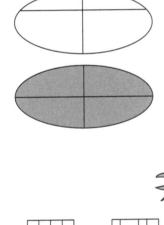

2.

3.

4.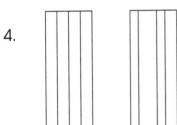

5.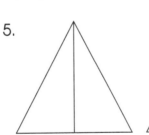

6.

7.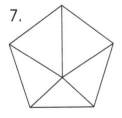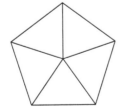

8.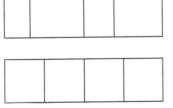

9.

Equal Parts

Look at the shapes. Each shape has **four** equal parts. Each part is $\frac{1}{4}$ or one quarter.

Write the fraction $\frac{1}{4}$ in each part.

1.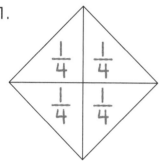

2.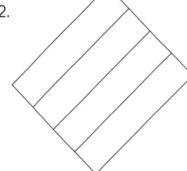

3.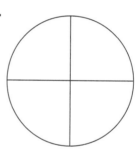

4.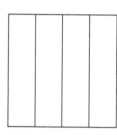

Color $\frac{1}{4}$ of each shape. The first one is done for you.

5.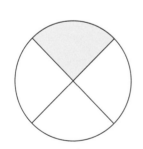

6.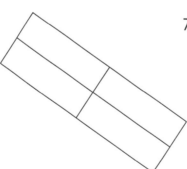

7.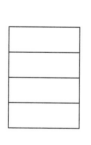

8.

9.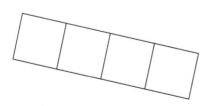

10.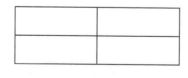

11.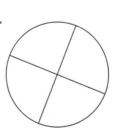

12.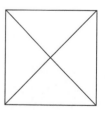

What Is a Fraction?

A fraction tells how many equal parts are in the whole object.

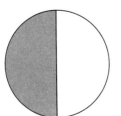 $\dfrac{1}{2}$  $\dfrac{1}{3}$ 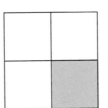 $\dfrac{1}{4}$

The bottom number of a fraction tells how many parts in all.

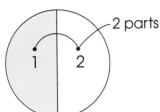 $\dfrac{1}{2}$ Parts in all

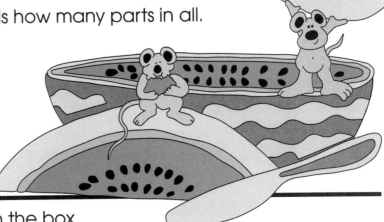

Count the parts. Write the number in the box.

1.
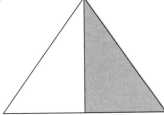 $\dfrac{1}{\boxed{}}$

2.
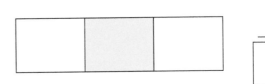 $\dfrac{1}{\boxed{}}$

3.
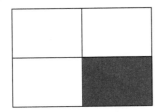 $\dfrac{1}{\boxed{}}$

4.
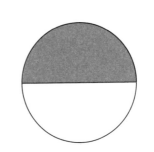 $\dfrac{1}{\boxed{}}$

5.
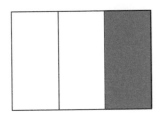 $\dfrac{1}{\boxed{}}$

6.
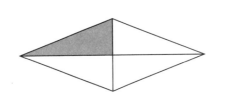 $\dfrac{1}{\boxed{}}$

Fractional Meaning–Bottom Number

More Fractions

A fraction tells how many parts of a whole are being used.
These fractions tell about the shaded part of each shape.

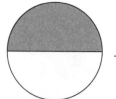 $\dfrac{1}{2}$ 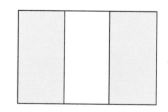 $\dfrac{2}{3}$ $\dfrac{3}{4}$

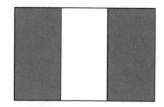 $\dfrac{2}{3}$ — Parts shaded

— Parts in all

Write the correct fraction for each shaded object.

1. $\dfrac{}{4}$

2. 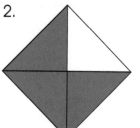 $\dfrac{}{4}$

3. 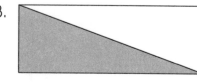 $\dfrac{}{2}$

4. 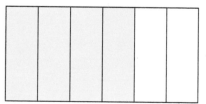 $\dfrac{}{6}$

5. 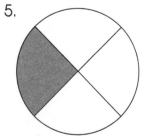 $\dfrac{}{4}$

6. 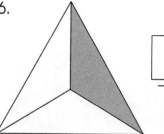 $\dfrac{}{3}$

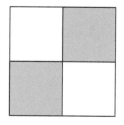

Pick the Fraction

Circle the correct fraction.

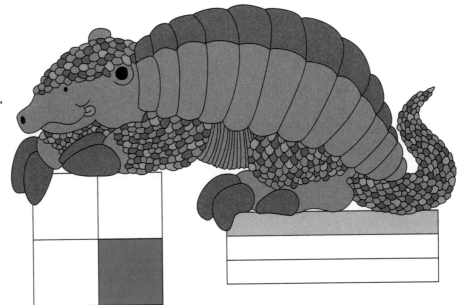

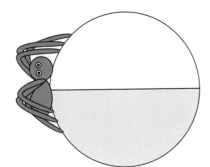

1. $\boxed{\dfrac{1}{2}}$ $\dfrac{1}{3}$ $\dfrac{1}{4}$

2. $\dfrac{1}{2}$ $\dfrac{1}{3}$ $\dfrac{1}{4}$

3. $\dfrac{1}{2}$ $\dfrac{1}{3}$ $\dfrac{1}{4}$

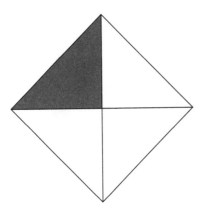

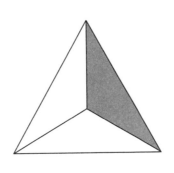

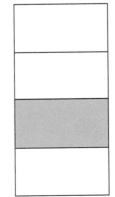

4. $\dfrac{1}{2}$ $\dfrac{1}{3}$ $\dfrac{1}{4}$

5. $\dfrac{1}{2}$ $\dfrac{1}{3}$ $\dfrac{1}{4}$

6. $\dfrac{1}{2}$ $\dfrac{1}{3}$ $\dfrac{1}{4}$

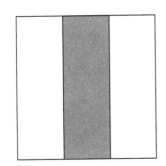

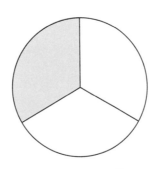

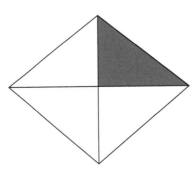

7. $\dfrac{1}{2}$ $\dfrac{1}{3}$ $\dfrac{1}{4}$

8. $\dfrac{1}{2}$ $\dfrac{1}{3}$ $\dfrac{1}{4}$

9. $\dfrac{1}{2}$ $\dfrac{1}{3}$ $\dfrac{1}{4}$

Pick the Fraction

Circle the correct fraction.

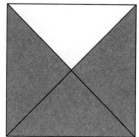

1.
$\frac{3}{4}$ $\frac{1}{4}$ $\frac{2}{3}$

2.
$\frac{2}{3}$ $\frac{1}{2}$ $\frac{1}{3}$

3.
$\frac{1}{8}$ $\frac{7}{8}$ $\frac{3}{8}$

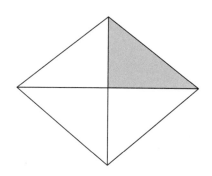

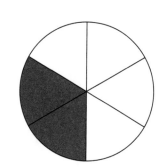

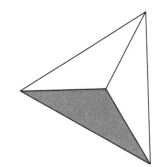

4.
$\frac{1}{8}$ $\frac{2}{3}$ $\frac{1}{4}$

5.
$\frac{1}{6}$ $\frac{1}{2}$ $\frac{2}{6}$

6.
$\frac{1}{4}$ $\frac{1}{3}$ $\frac{1}{2}$

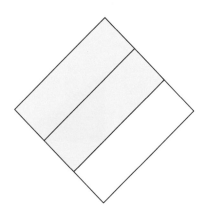

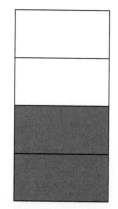

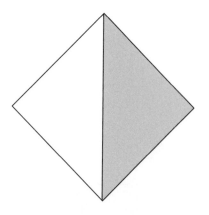

7.
$\frac{1}{3}$ $\frac{2}{3}$ $\frac{1}{2}$

8.
$\frac{3}{4}$ $\frac{1}{4}$ $\frac{2}{4}$

9.
$\frac{1}{3}$ $\frac{1}{2}$ $\frac{3}{4}$

More Fractions

Color the objects to show the fraction.

1.

$\dfrac{1}{2}$

2.

$\dfrac{3}{4}$

3.

$\dfrac{2}{3}$

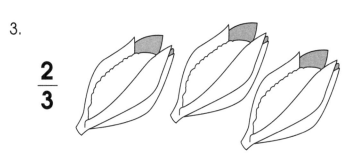

4.

$\dfrac{7}{8}$

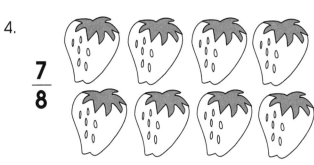

5.

$\dfrac{2}{5}$

6.

$\dfrac{1}{4}$

7.

$\dfrac{1}{8}$

8.

$\dfrac{3}{6}$

More Fractions

   $\dfrac{1}{3}$

Circle the objects that equal each fraction.

1. $\dfrac{1}{4}$

2. $\dfrac{2}{5}$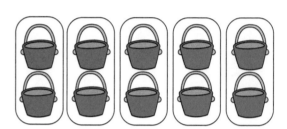

3. $\dfrac{1}{2}$

4. $\dfrac{1}{4}$

5. $\dfrac{1}{3}$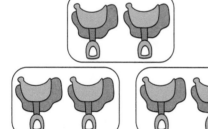

6. $\dfrac{3}{6}$

7. $\dfrac{3}{4}$

8. $\dfrac{1}{2}$

What I Learned About Fractions

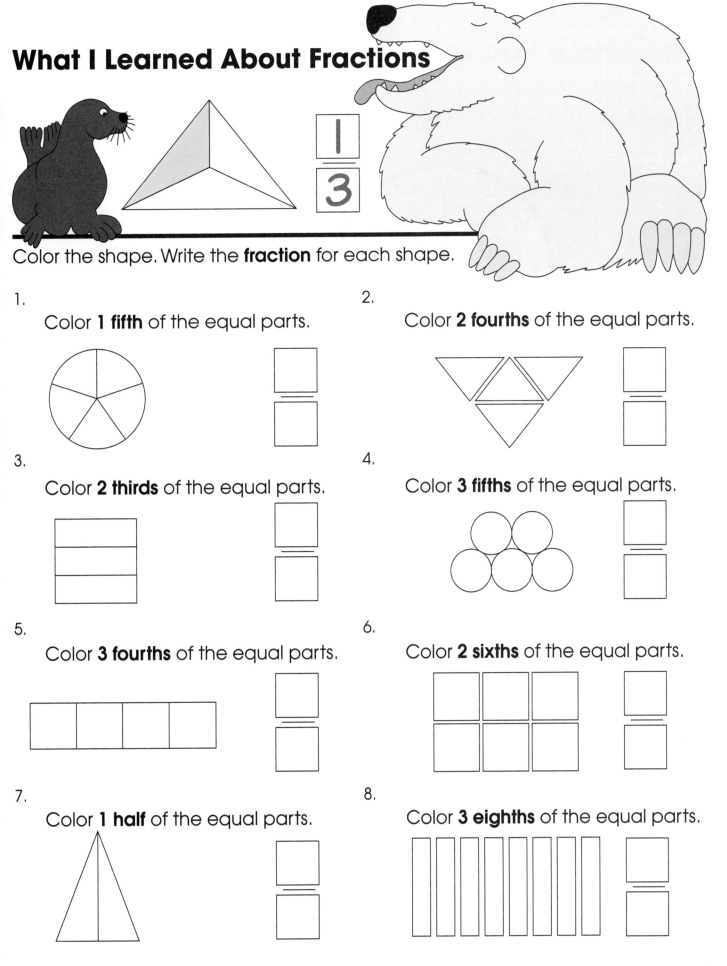

Color the shape. Write the **fraction** for each shape.

1.
Color **1 fifth** of the equal parts.

2.
Color **2 fourths** of the equal parts.

3.
Color **2 thirds** of the equal parts.

4.
Color **3 fifths** of the equal parts.

5.
Color **3 fourths** of the equal parts.

6.
Color **2 sixths** of the equal parts.

7.
Color **1 half** of the equal parts.

8.
Color **3 eighths** of the equal parts.

Telling Time: Hours

A clock has two hands. The short hand shows the hours.
When the long hand points to **12**, we say **o'clock**.

The time is **2 o'clock**.
2:00

Read the hour hand first. Then read the minute hand. Write the time.

1. _____2_____ o'clock

_____2:00_____

2. _____ o'clock

____:____

3. _____ o'clock

____:____

4. _____ o'clock

____:____

5. _____ o'clock

____:____

6. _____ o'clock

____:____

Telling Time: Half Hours

The long hand tells the minutes. When the minute hand points to the **6**, we say it is half past the hour. The minute hand is halfway around the clock. The hour hand is between **2** and **3**.

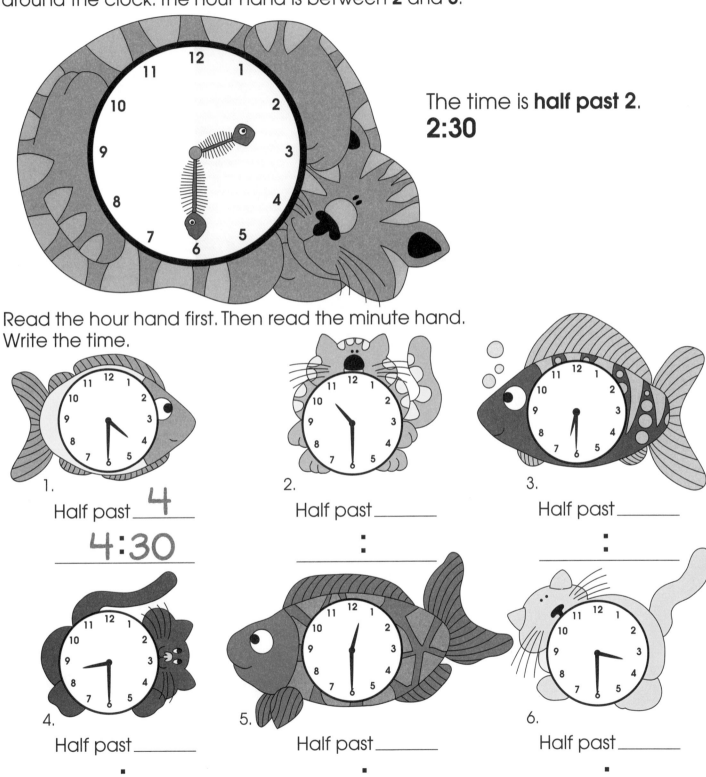

The time is **half past 2**.
2:30

Read the hour hand first. Then read the minute hand. Write the time.

1.
Half past __4__

4:30

2.
Half past_____

__ : __

3.
Half past_____

__ : __

4.
Half past_____

__ : __

5.
Half past_____

__ : __

6.
Half past_____

__ : __

Telling Time

Write the time.

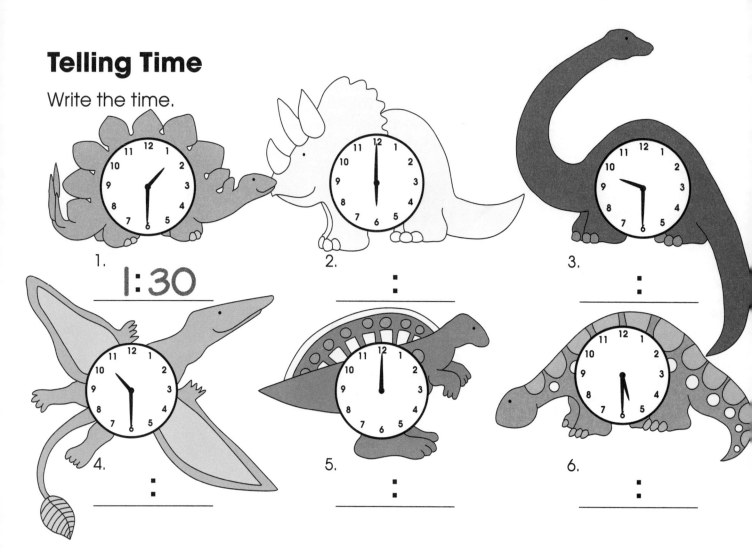

1. 1:30

2. __:__

3. __:__

4. __:__

5. __:__

6. __:__

Draw hands to show the time.

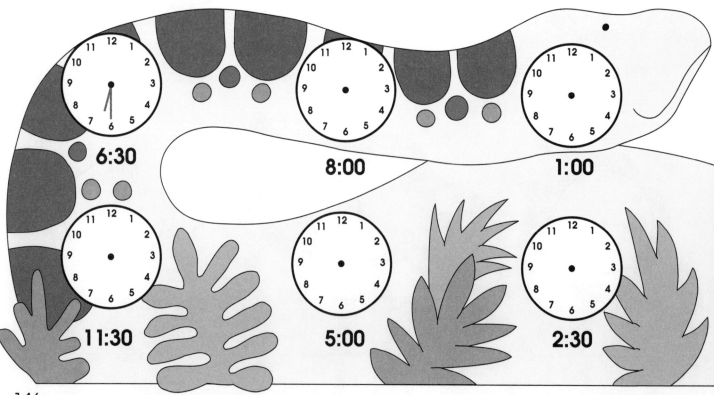

6:30

8:00

1:00

11:30

5:00

2:30

Telling Time: Minutes

The minute hand of the clock takes **5** minutes to move from one number to the next. Count by **5**'s starting from **12**.

Write the minutes on each line.

5

25

How many minutes in an hour? _____

Telling Time: Quarter Past

When the minute hand points to the **3**, it is one quarter of the way around the clock. It is quarter past the hour. The hour hand is a little past **2:00**.

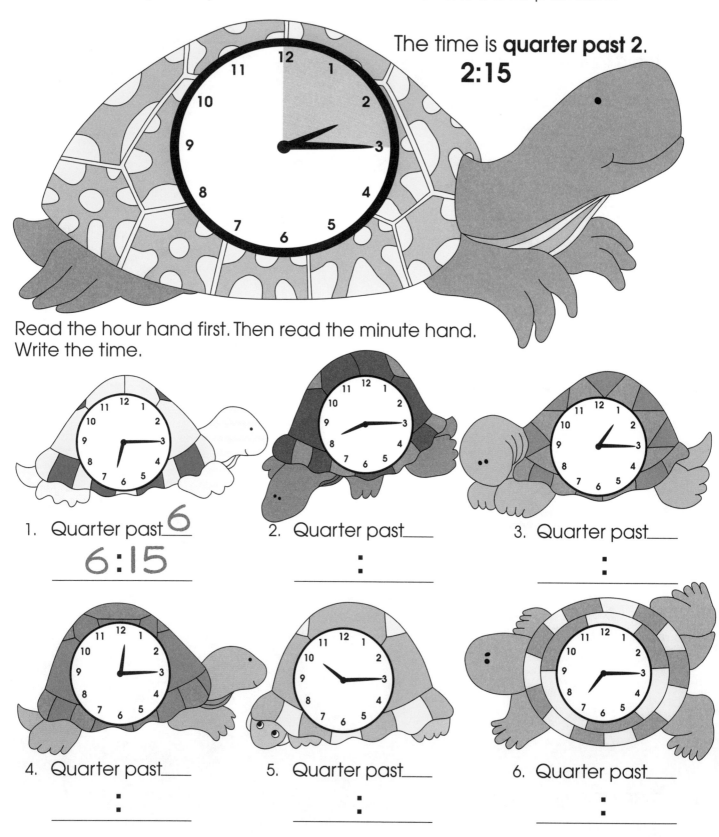

The time is **quarter past 2**.
2:15

Read the hour hand first. Then read the minute hand. Write the time.

1. Quarter past 6

6:15

2. Quarter past____

___:___

3. Quarter past____

___:___

4. Quarter past____

___:___

5. Quarter past____

___:___

6. Quarter past____

___:___

Telling Time: Quarter To

When the minute hand points to **9**, it is one quarter to the hour.
The hour hand is almost to the **3**.

The time is **quarter to 3**.
2:45

Read the hour hand first. Then read the minute hand.
Write the time.

1. Quarter to ___4___

___3:45___

2. Quarter to _____

___ : ___

3. Quarter to _____

___ : ___

4. Quarter to _____

___ : ___

5. Quarter to _____

___ : ___

6. Quarter to _____

___ : ___

Telling Time

Write the time.

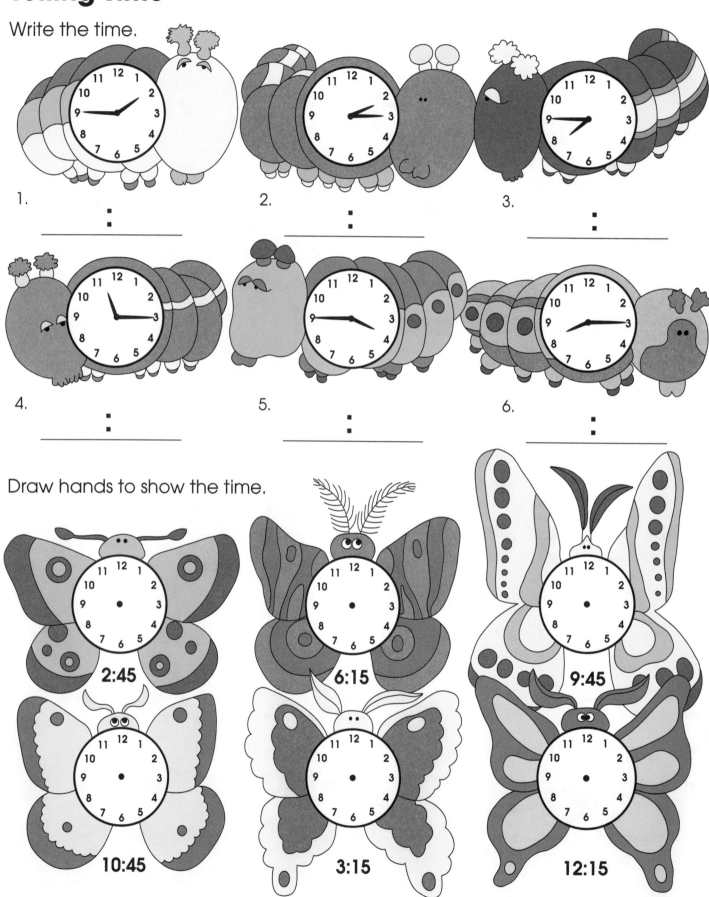

1. ___:___

2. ___:___

3. ___:___

4. ___:___

5. ___:___

6. ___:___

Draw hands to show the time.

2:45

6:15

9:45

10:45

3:15

12:15

Telling Time: Minutes

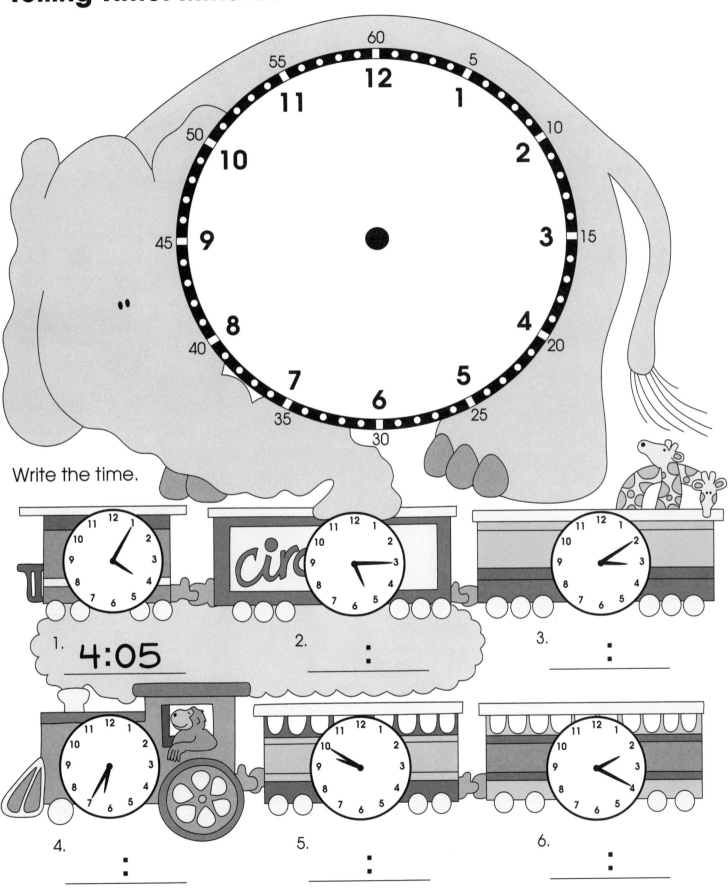

Write the time.

1. **4:05**

2. _____ : _____

3. _____ : _____

4. _____ : _____

5. _____ : _____

6. _____ : _____

Telling Time

Write the time.

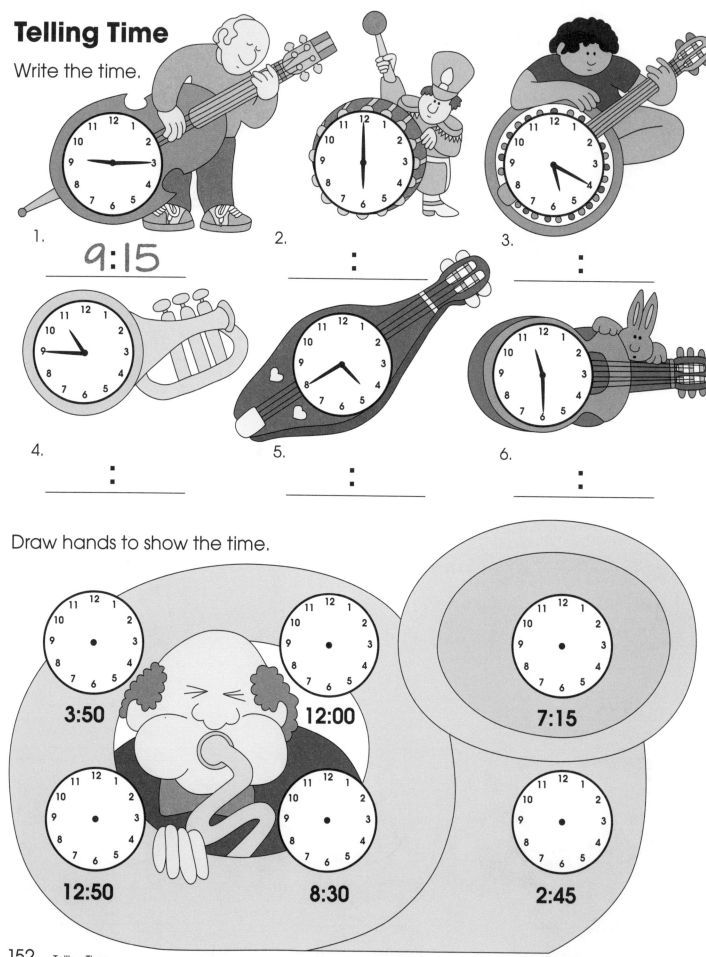

1. 9:15

2. :

3. :

4. :

5. :

6. :

Draw hands to show the time.

3:50

12:00

7:15

12:50

8:30

2:45

Matching Numerals to Objects

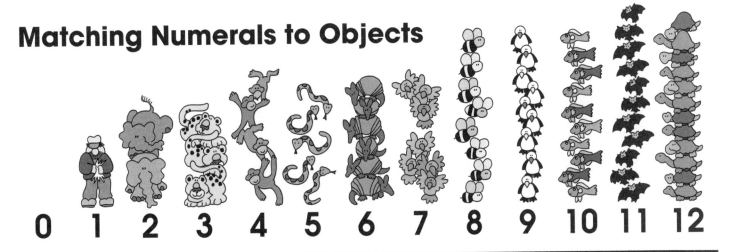

0   1   2   3   4   5   6   7   8   9   10   11   12

Circle the numeral that tells how many there are.

2   3

1   2

5   6

6   7

5   6

3   4

0   1

8   9

Writing Numerals

Trace the numerals.

0 1 2 3 4
5 6 7 8 9
10 11 12

I did it!
So can you.

Write the numerals from **0** to **12** in order.

Writing Numerals for Objects

How many objects are in each set?
Write the numeral.

1. _____

2. _____

Draw **10** 🐟 .

Draw **7** 🐍 .

Draw **2** 🐻 .

Draw **11** 🐝 .

Which Is Greater Than?

In math, **greater** means **more than**.
5 is **greater** than **3**.

Circle the set that is **greater**.

1.

2.

3.

Make a set of to show **1** more than **3**.

How many ? _____

Concept of Greater Than

Which Is Less Than?

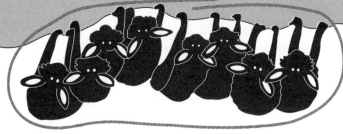 

In math, **less** means **not as many**.
8 is **less** than **9**.

Circle the set that is **less**.

1.

2.

3.

Make a set of to show **1** less than **10**.

How many  ? _____

Concept of Less Than   157

Let's Count to 100!

Count to **100**.
Write the missing numerals to count from **1** to **100**.

1	2								10
11	12								
					26				
		33							
				45					
							58		60
			64						
	72								
						87			
									100

Count by **2**'s. Color those squares **yellow**.

Which Numerals Are Missing?

Write the missing numerals in each row.

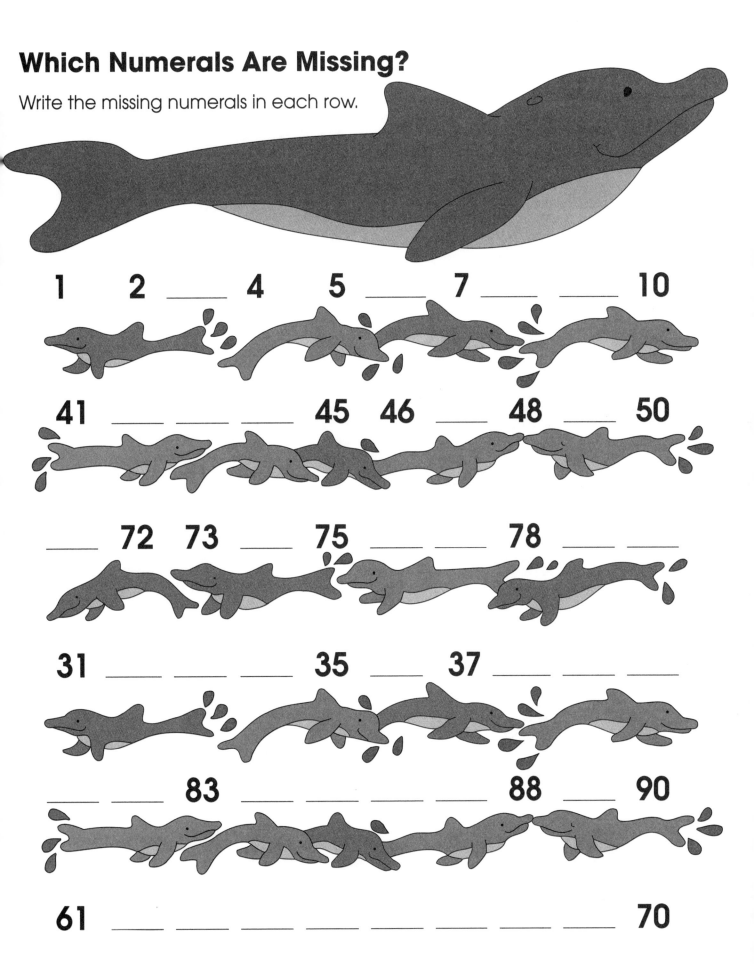

1   2 ___   4   5 ___   7 ___ ___   10

41 ___ ___ ___   45   46 ___   48 ___   50

___   72   73 ___   75 ___ ___   78 ___ ___

31 ___ ___ ___   35 ___   37 ___ ___ ___

___   83 ___ ___ ___ ___   88 ___   90

61 ___ ___ ___ ___ ___ ___ ___ ___   70

Adding to Find the Sum

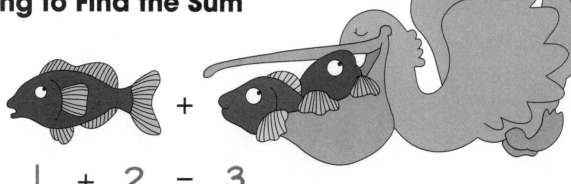

$$\underline{1} + \underline{2} = \underline{3}$$

Write a number sentence about each picture.
Find the **sum**.
The **sum** tells how many in all.

1.

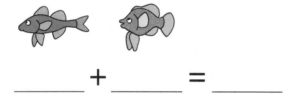

_____ + _____ = _____

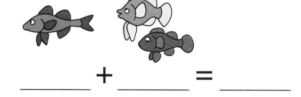

_____ + _____ = _____

2.

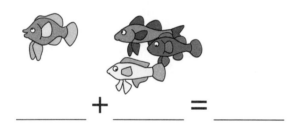

_____ + _____ = _____

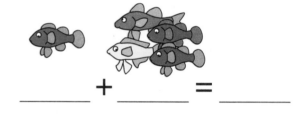

_____ + _____ = _____

3.

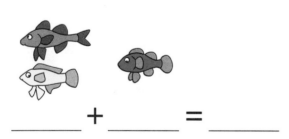

_____ + _____ = _____

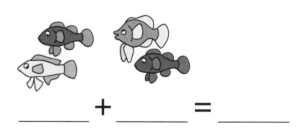

_____ + _____ = _____

4.

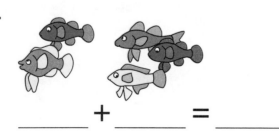

_____ + _____ = _____

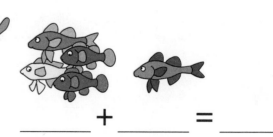

_____ + _____ = _____

More Adding

It's easy!

$$2 + 1 = 3$$

Write a number sentence about each picture.
Find the **sum**.

1.  ___ + ___ = ___

2. 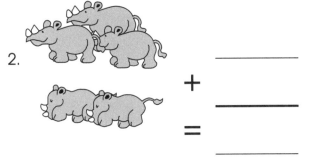 ___ + ___ = ___

3. 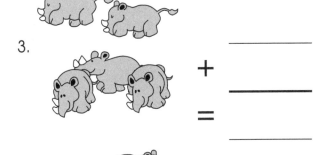 ___ + ___ = ___

4. 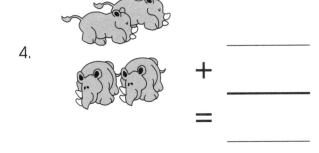 ___ + ___ = ___

Addition Fun

Find the **sum**.
Color the picture.

$1 + 2 =$ _____ **Brown**

$1 + 0 =$ _____ **Red**

$1 + 1 =$ _____ **Yellow**

$3 + 1 =$ _____ **Green**

$3 + 3 =$ _____ **Blue**

$2 + 3 =$ _____ **Black**

Subtracting to Find the Difference

$$\underline{}\ 5\ \underline{} - \underline{}\ 2\ \underline{} = \underline{}\ 3\ \underline{}$$

Write a number sentence about each picture.
Write the **difference**.
The **difference** tells how many are left.

1.

_____ − _____ = _____

2.

_____ − _____ = _____

3.
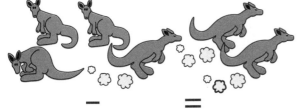

_____ − _____ = _____

4.

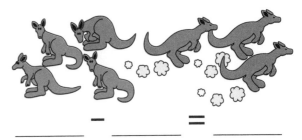

_____ − _____ = _____

More Subtracting

$$-\ 3$$
$$\underline{1}$$
$$=\ 2$$

Write a number sentence about each picture.
Find the **difference**.

1.

$$-\ \underline{\qquad}$$
$$=\ \underline{\qquad}$$

$$-\ \underline{\qquad}$$
$$=\ \underline{\qquad}$$

2.

$$-\ \underline{\qquad}$$
$$=\ \underline{\qquad}$$

$$-\ \underline{\qquad}$$
$$=\ \underline{\qquad}$$

3.

$$-\ \underline{\qquad}$$
$$=\ \underline{\qquad}$$

$$-\ \underline{\qquad}$$
$$=\ \underline{\qquad}$$

4.
$$-\ \underline{\qquad}$$
$$=\ \underline{\qquad}$$

$$-\ \underline{\qquad}$$
$$=\ \underline{\qquad}$$

Subtraction Equations

Find the **difference**.
Color the picture.

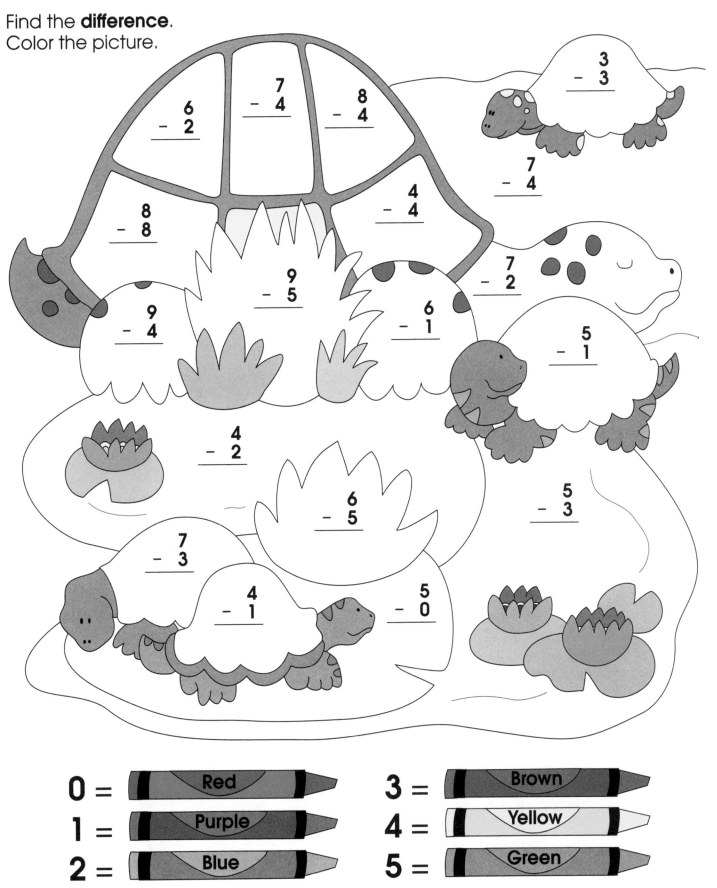

$$\begin{array}{r} 6 \\ -\ 2 \\ \hline \end{array}$$

$$\begin{array}{r} 7 \\ -\ 4 \\ \hline \end{array}$$

$$\begin{array}{r} 8 \\ -\ 4 \\ \hline \end{array}$$

$$\begin{array}{r} 3 \\ -\ 3 \\ \hline \end{array}$$

$$\begin{array}{r} 7 \\ -\ 4 \\ \hline \end{array}$$

$$\begin{array}{r} 8 \\ -\ 8 \\ \hline \end{array}$$

$$\begin{array}{r} 4 \\ -\ 4 \\ \hline \end{array}$$

$$\begin{array}{r} 9 \\ -\ 5 \\ \hline \end{array}$$

$$\begin{array}{r} 7 \\ -\ 2 \\ \hline \end{array}$$

$$\begin{array}{r} 9 \\ -\ 4 \\ \hline \end{array}$$

$$\begin{array}{r} 6 \\ -\ 1 \\ \hline \end{array}$$

$$\begin{array}{r} 5 \\ -\ 1 \\ \hline \end{array}$$

$$\begin{array}{r} 4 \\ -\ 2 \\ \hline \end{array}$$

$$\begin{array}{r} 6 \\ -\ 5 \\ \hline \end{array}$$

$$\begin{array}{r} 5 \\ -\ 3 \\ \hline \end{array}$$

$$\begin{array}{r} 7 \\ -\ 3 \\ \hline \end{array}$$

$$\begin{array}{r} 4 \\ -\ 1 \\ \hline \end{array}$$

$$\begin{array}{r} 5 \\ -\ 0 \\ \hline \end{array}$$

0 = Red

1 = Purple

2 = Blue

3 = Brown

4 = Yellow

5 = Green

Adding to Find the Sum

Fill in the table by finding the **sum**.
Color your answers.

+	0	1	2	3	4	5
0	0					
1						
2					5	
3		4				
4						
5						

2 + 3 = 5

0 = Red
1 = Purple
2 = Blue
3 = Orange
4 = Yellow
5 = Green

Addition Practice

Number lines can help you find the **sum**.

$$
\begin{array}{r} 7 \\ +\ 3 \\ \hline 10 \end{array}
$$

Count **3** numbers more than **7**.

Use the number line.

1.
$$
\begin{array}{r} 5 \\ +\ 2 \\ \hline \end{array}
\qquad
\begin{array}{r} 6 \\ +\ 3 \\ \hline \end{array}
\qquad
\begin{array}{r} 5 \\ +\ 3 \\ \hline \end{array}
\qquad
\begin{array}{r} 4 \\ +\ 4 \\ \hline \end{array}
$$

2.
$$
\begin{array}{r} 7 \\ +\ 5 \\ \hline \end{array}
\qquad
\begin{array}{r} 3 \\ +\ 4 \\ \hline \end{array}
\qquad
\begin{array}{r} 7 \\ +\ 2 \\ \hline \end{array}
\qquad
\begin{array}{r} 9 \\ +\ 2 \\ \hline \end{array}
$$

3.
$$
\begin{array}{r} 6 \\ +\ 2 \\ \hline \end{array}
\qquad
\begin{array}{r} 7 \\ +\ 4 \\ \hline \end{array}
\qquad
\begin{array}{r} 5 \\ +\ 5 \\ \hline \end{array}
\qquad
\begin{array}{r} 8 \\ +\ 4 \\ \hline \end{array}
$$

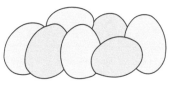

Adding Made Easy

 Get it?

Add **1** to each numeral.
Write the answer.

8   _9_

0 1 2 3 4 5 6 7 8 9 10 11 12

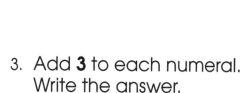

1. Add **1** to each numeral.
Write the answer.

6   _____

4   _____

7   _____

9   _____

2. Add **2** to each numeral.
Write the answer.

5   _____

2   _____

8   _____

6   _____

Good Job!

3. Add **3** to each numeral.
Write the answer.

3   _____

6   _____

2   _____

9   _____

4. Add **4** to each numeral.
Write the answer.

5   _____

8   _____

4   _____

1   _____

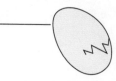

Subtraction Practice

$10 - 3 = \underline{7}$

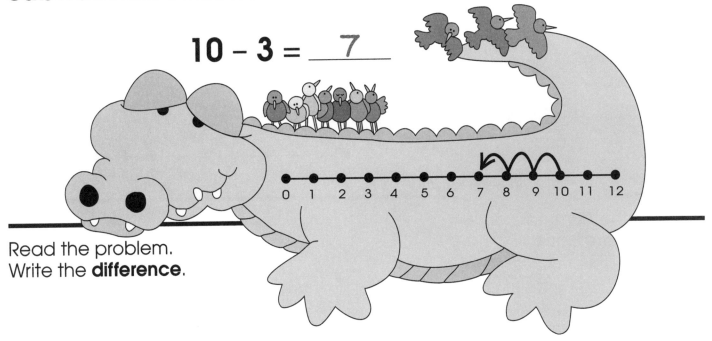

Read the problem.
Write the **difference**.

1. $10 - 2 = \underline{}$

$10 - 8 = \underline{}$

2. $9 - 3 = \underline{}$

$9 - 6 = \underline{}$

3. $12 - 5 = \underline{}$

$12 - 7 = \underline{}$

4. $11 - 4 = \underline{}$

$11 - 7 = \underline{}$

More Subtraction Practice

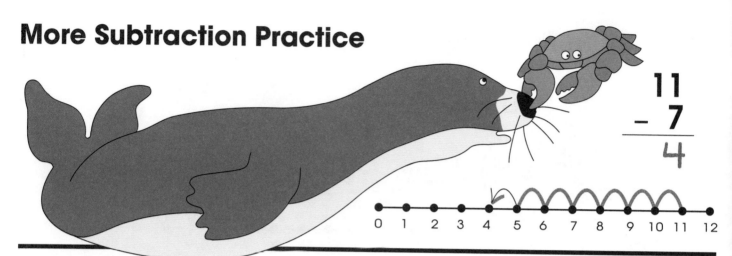

$$\begin{array}{r} 11 \\ -\ 7 \\ \hline 4 \end{array}$$

Subtract the numerals.
Write the **difference**.

1. $\begin{array}{r} 8 \\ -\ 5 \\ \hline \end{array}$ $\begin{array}{r} 10 \\ -\ 4 \\ \hline \end{array}$ $\begin{array}{r} 9 \\ -\ 5 \\ \hline \end{array}$

2. $\begin{array}{r} 9 \\ -\ 6 \\ \hline \end{array}$ $\begin{array}{r} 8 \\ -\ 3 \\ \hline \end{array}$ $\begin{array}{r} 10 \\ -\ 2 \\ \hline \end{array}$

3. $\begin{array}{r} 9 \\ -\ 4 \\ \hline \end{array}$ $\begin{array}{r} 11 \\ -\ 2 \\ \hline \end{array}$ $\begin{array}{r} 12 \\ -\ 7 \\ \hline \end{array}$

4. $\begin{array}{r} 12 \\ -\ 5 \\ \hline \end{array}$ $\begin{array}{r} 11 \\ -\ 4 \\ \hline \end{array}$ $\begin{array}{r} 12 \\ -\ 8 \\ \hline \end{array}$

Adding and Subtracting

Follow the path around the animals that like water.
Find the **sums** and **differences**.

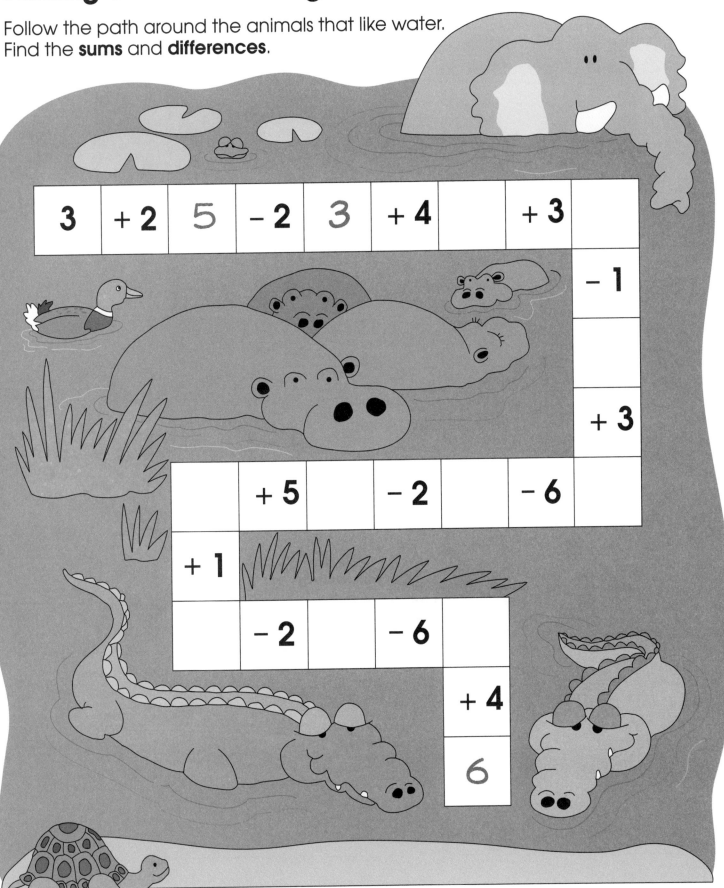

| 3 | + 2 | 5 | − 2 | 3 | + 4 | | + 3 | |

Counting Ones and Tens

Start at the ▲. Connect the dots counting by **ones** to **21**.
Start at the ■. Connect the dots counting by **tens** to **100**.

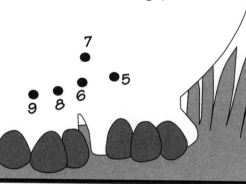

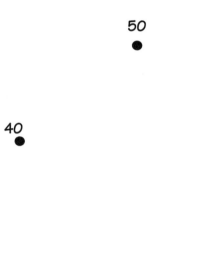

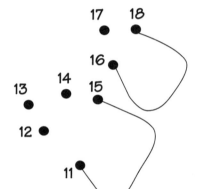
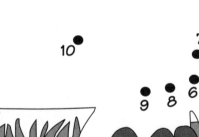
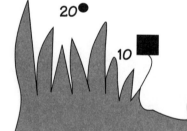

Write the missing numerals.

__10__ _____ __30__ _____ _____

_____ __70__ _____ _____ _____

Sets of Ten

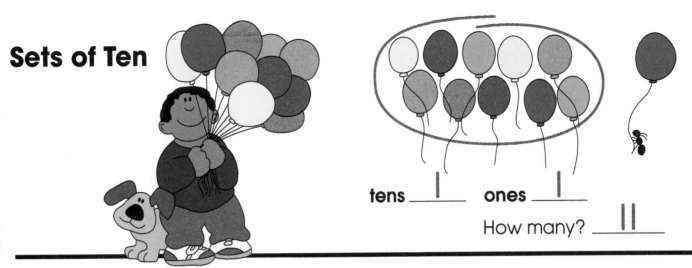

tens _____ ones _____

How many? _____

Count the number of objects.
Circle the objects in sets of **ten**.

1.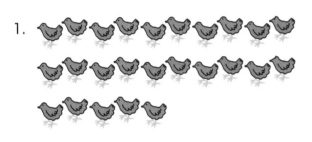

_____ tens _____ ones

How many? _____

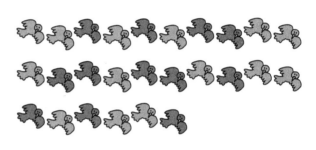

_____ tens _____ ones

How many? _____

2.

_____ tens _____ ones

How many? _____

_____ tens _____ ones

How many? _____

3.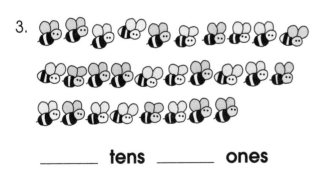

_____ tens _____ ones

How many? _____

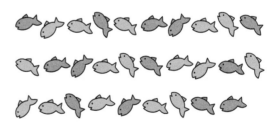

_____ tens _____ ones

How many? _____

Let's Learn More About Tens and Ones!

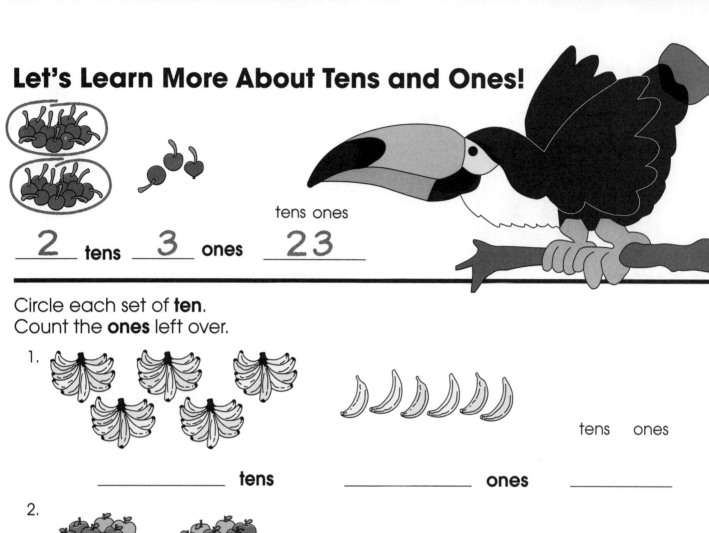

__2__ tens __3__ ones

tens ones

__23__

Circle each set of **ten**.
Count the **ones** left over.

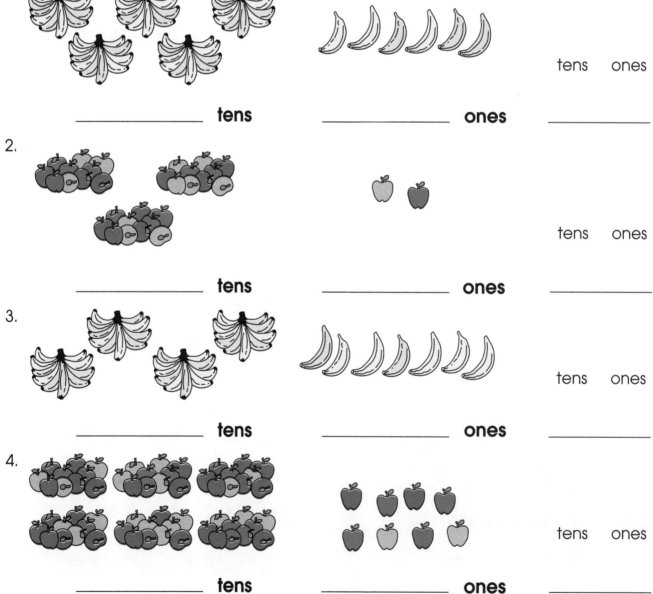

1.
_____ **tens**   _____ **ones**   tens   ones
_____

2.
_____ **tens**   _____ **ones**   tens   ones
_____

3.
_____ **tens**   _____ **ones**   tens   ones
_____

4.
_____ **tens**   _____ **ones**   tens   ones
_____

More Practice Using Tens and Ones

Read each number.
Write how many **tens** and how many **ones**.

	tens	ones
1. **25**	2	5
43	___	___
28	___	___
30	___	___
54	___	___
65	___	___

	tens	ones
2. **17**	___	___
71	___	___
66	___	___
19	___	___
81	___	___
40	___	___

Place Value–Tens and Ones

More Practice Using Tens and Ones

Write the correct numeral.

1. **2** tens and **6** ones = <u>26</u>   **4** tens and **5** ones = _____

2. **4** tens and **1** one = _____   **5** tens and **3** ones = _____

3. **7** tens and **0** ones = _____   **1** ten and **9** ones = _____

4. **2** tens and **5** ones = _____   **6** tens and **4** ones = _____

5. **0** tens and **8** ones = _____   **9** tens and **2** ones = _____

6. **8** tens and **6** ones = _____   **5** tens and **0** ones = _____

7. **3** tens and **7** ones = _____   **2** tens and **2** ones = _____

Before and After

Read each numeral.
Write the numeral that comes **before**.

1. _17_ **18**   _____ **33**

2. _____ **24**   _____ **67**

3. _____ **81**   _____ **30**

4. _____ **45**   _____ **27**

Read each numeral.
Write the numeral that comes **after**.

5. **22** _23_   **11** _____

6. **18** _____   **37** _____

7. **27** _____   **6** _____

8. **38** _____   **69** _____

Concept of Before and After   177

Greater Than and Less Than

Circle the numeral that is **greater**.

1. (23) 14   50 48   25 31

2. 21 19   35 27   10 15

3. 18 10   13 31   43 34

Circle the numeral that is **less**.

4. 55 (48)   25 71   23 36

5. 62 59   18 13   25 31

6. 58 69 44 54   78 82

Greater and Less Than Using Tens and Ones

Do You Add or Subtract?

Write the **sum** or the **difference**.

$$\begin{array}{r} 12 \\ -\ 3 \\ \hline \end{array}$$

$$\begin{array}{r} 7 \\ +\ 3 \\ \hline \end{array}$$

$$\begin{array}{r} 10 \\ -\ 4 \\ \hline \end{array}$$

$$\begin{array}{r} 8 \\ +\ 2 \\ \hline \end{array}$$

$$\begin{array}{r} 10 \\ -\ 8 \\ \hline \end{array}$$

$$\begin{array}{r} 12 \\ -\ 4 \\ \hline \end{array}$$

$$\begin{array}{r} 12 \\ -\ 7 \\ \hline \end{array}$$

$$\begin{array}{r} 5 \\ +\ 3 \\ \hline \end{array}$$

$$\begin{array}{r} 1 \\ +11 \\ \hline \end{array}$$

$$\begin{array}{r} 9 \\ -\ 7 \\ \hline \end{array}$$

$$\begin{array}{r} 10 \\ -\ 3 \\ \hline \end{array}$$

$$\begin{array}{r} 11 \\ -\ 4 \\ \hline \end{array}$$

$$\begin{array}{r} 12 \\ -\ 6 \\ \hline \end{array}$$

$$\begin{array}{r} 7 \\ +\ 2 \\ \hline \end{array}$$

$$\begin{array}{r} 0 \\ +\ 4 \\ \hline \end{array}$$

$$\begin{array}{r} 5 \\ +\ 6 \\ \hline \end{array}$$

Do You Add or Subtract?

Write the **sum** or the **difference**.

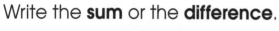

1.
$$\begin{array}{r} 6 \\ +\ 3 \\ \hline \end{array}$$
$$\begin{array}{r} 11 \\ -\ 6 \\ \hline \end{array}$$
$$\begin{array}{r} 8 \\ +\ 4 \\ \hline \end{array}$$
$$\begin{array}{r} 11 \\ -\ 5 \\ \hline \end{array}$$

2.
$$\begin{array}{r} 12 \\ -\ 0 \\ \hline \end{array}$$
$$\begin{array}{r} 11 \\ -\ 3 \\ \hline \end{array}$$
$$\begin{array}{r} 5 \\ +\ 5 \\ \hline \end{array}$$
$$\begin{array}{r} 0 \\ +12 \\ \hline \end{array}$$

3.
$$\begin{array}{r} 9 \\ -\ 5 \\ \hline \end{array}$$
$$\begin{array}{r} 12 \\ -\ 4 \\ \hline \end{array}$$
$$\begin{array}{r} 10 \\ -\ 4 \\ \hline \end{array}$$
$$\begin{array}{r} 12 \\ -\ 3 \\ \hline \end{array}$$

4.
$$\begin{array}{r} 10 \\ -\ 5 \\ \hline \end{array}$$
$$\begin{array}{r} 9 \\ +\ 2 \\ \hline \end{array}$$
$$\begin{array}{r} 0 \\ +\ 5 \\ \hline \end{array}$$
$$\begin{array}{r} 4 \\ +\ 4 \\ \hline \end{array}$$

Which Problems Give the Right Answer?

Circle the problems that give the right answer.

1. **9**   (10 – 1)   (2 + 7)   (8 + 1)   3 + 5   11 – 3

2. **5**   3 + 3   6 – 1   5 + 1   5 + 0   9 – 4

3. **8**   10 – 2   4 + 4   6 + 3   2 + 6   12 – 6

4. **10**   12 – 3   6 + 4   7 + 3   4 + 5   11 – 1

5. **12**   4 + 7   12 – 0   8 + 4   7 + 5   6 + 5

6. **6**   3 + 3   12 – 6   5 + 1   9 + 3   11 – 4

7. **11**   6 + 4   9 + 2   5 + 6   7 + 5   8 + 3

8. **7**   7 + 0   11 – 4   4 + 3   2 + 6   12 – 6

Race to the Monkey House

Take turns giving the answer to every other problem. The player who has the most correct answers wins.

3 tens + **7** ones = _____

Start

```
   3
+  4
```

```
   10
+   6
```

```
   12
-   7
```

```
   11
+   5
```

```
   10
+   8
```

```
   18
+   1
```

```
   6
-  3
```

```
    9
-  [ ]
    6
```

```
   8
+  3
```

```
   15
-  [ ]
   10
```

```
   11
-  [ ]
    7
```

```
   8
+  2
```

```
   8
+  4
```

```
   12
-  [ ]
    8
```

```
   12
-   5
```

```
    6
+  [ ]
   14
```

```
   7
-  5
```

```
   10
-   3
```

```
   13
-  [ ]
    7
```

```
   10
+  [ ]
   12
```

```
   9
+  3
```

```
   12
-   3
```

```
   11
-   7
```

```
   12
-  [ ]
    5
```

```
   12
-   4
```

```
   9
+  2
```

```
   20
+  10
```

Finish

6 tens + **4** ones = _____

```
_____  85  _____
```

```
    6
+  [ ]
   12
```

182   Addition/Subtraction

©School Zone Publishing Company

Puzzling Names

Write the first letter of each picture.
Read the animal name.
Write the number in its circle.

_____ _____ _____ _____

1. _____

_____ _____ _____ _____ _____ _____

2. _____

_____ _____ _____ _____ _____

3. _____

Try This!

Make a puzzle! You need nature magazines to cut up,
scissors, glue, and heavy paper or cardboard.
1. Cut out a large picture of an animal.
2. Glue the picture on cardboard or heavy paper.
3. Cut the picture into puzzle pieces.
4. Put your puzzle back together.

We're on Our Way!

Help the Romeros and their friends get to the zoo.
Look at the names of places they will pass.
Number the words in ABC order.
Then follow the path from 1 to 8.

GROCERY

HOSPITAL

FIREHOUSE

BANK

Try This!

Draw a map. Show how to get from your house to a
favorite place. Show the streets on which you travel.
Include the places you pass.

POST OFFICE

SCHOOL

TOYS

ZIPPITY ZOO

Which animal knows its ABCs?

The alpha-bat!

What's Up at the Zoo?

Look at the zoo map and the map key.
Then follow the directions.

1. Draw a line to show a way to the Snake House.

2. Draw a ▢ to show where you can see a 🐯.

3. Draw a △ to show where you can see a 🦆.

Write the name of the place you would go first.

4. _____

Write **yes** or **no**.

5. Can you see an  in the zoo? _____

6. Can you see a in the zoo? _____

7. Can you see a in the zoo? _____

Water World

Say **a**, **e**, **i**, **o**, and **u**. These are the long vowels.
Then say the words on the fish.
Color the long vowel fish **orange**.

The other words have short vowel sounds.
Color the short vowel fish **green**.

Help the squid get to her cave.
Draw a line to connect the long vowel fish.

Honey Bear

Honey Bear is running in circles!
She is looking for words with short vowel sounds.
Start at the arrow. Write eight words you find.
Then go the other way. Say the words.

1. _____

2. _____

3. _____

4. _____

5. _____

6. _____

7. _____

8. _____

Try This!

Have an adult help you make this honey of a treat.

2 apples, cored & peeled	1/2 cup walnut pieces
1/2 cup raisins	1/4 cup apple juice
1 tablespoon honey	8 graham crackers

1. Chop the apples, walnuts, and raisins.
2. Stir in the juice and honey.
3. Spread on crackers. Eat!

Phonics—Short Vowels

A Cool Rhyme

Read the rhyme.
Then draw a line under each number word.

Penguin Pals

Five little penguin pals resting on the shore.

One took a dip, and then there were four.

Four little penguin pals walking by the sea.

One little slip, and then there were three.

Three little penguin pals with nothing to do.

One little trip, and then there were two.

Two little penguin pals looking for fun.

One little flip, and then there was one.

One little penguin all alone.

He jumped in too, and now there are none!

Write the words that rhyme with **tip**.
Say other words that rhyme with **tip**.

1. _____

2. _____

3. _____

4. _____

Quackers Pond

Look at the pond. Write how many of each.

1. _____

2. _____

3. _____

4. _____

5. _____

6. _____

7. Draw 10 in the pond.

Sneaky Snakes

Write an **s** blend to finish each picture name. Choose from these.

st   sl   sk   sp
sn   sw

1. _____ ake

2. _____ an

3. _____ ider

4. _____ unk

5. _____ ug

6. _____ arfish

Circle words with **s** blends in the puzzle.

```
x  b  s  k  u  n  k
v  s  t  o  p  s  g
s  w  a  n  g  n  s
f  t  r  y  c  o  l
t  u  f  z  j  w  u
s  p  i  d  e  r  g
y  o  s  n  a  k  e
p  q  h  s  n  a  p
```

sn sl st sp sw sk

Try This!

Play a blend game. You need six paper cups and a pen. Label each cup with one blend: sn, sl, st, sp, sw, sk. Line up the cups on a table. Toss a softball or beanbag toy at the cups. For each cup you knock over, say a word that begins with the blend.

Desert Trail

Follow the path through the desert.
Add numerals to write the **sums**.
Subtract numerals to write the **differences**.

| 2 | +2 | | -1 | | +3 |

-1

| | -3 | | +3 | | +1 |

+4

| | -2 | | +3 | |

-5

Where Are the Animals?

Where are the animals on the Desert Trail?
Finish each sentence with a word below.

over   under   in   across   on

1. The roadrunner  runs **under** the  .

2. The lizard  sleeps _____ the  .

3. The jackrabbit  leaps _____ the  .

4. The snake  glides _____ the _____ .

5. The owl sits _____ the  .

Try This!

Play a game of Simon Says with family members or friends. Use the words from the oval on this page as you play.

We Work at the Zoo

Here are four people who work at Zippity Zoo.
Circle the name in each sentence.

Remember—A person's name begins with a capital letter.

Jan helps sick animals.   Bob keeps animal homes clean.

Chan teaches sea animals.   Lisa feeds hungry animals.

Write the correct name under each picture.

1. _____   2. _____

3. _____   4. _____

To make dough names, you need 1 cup peanut butter, 1 cup honey, and 2 cups powdered milk.

1. Wash your hands.
2. Mix the ingredients in a bowl.
3. Add more milk if the dough is too sticky.

4. Form the dough into the letters of your name.
5. Eat your name!

The names of special places begin with capital letters.
Zippity Zoo is a special place.
Zippity and **Zoo** begin with capital letters.
Circle the name of the special place in each sentence.

1. Parrots  live in Jungle World .

2. Ducks swim in Quackers Pond  .

3. Deer run in Zebra Park  .

4. Monkeys make noise on Monkey Island .

Look back at pages 186 and 187. Write the name of the special place bears live.

Big Cat Country

A word can name one. lion

A word can name more than one. lions

Many words add **s** to name more than one.

Write a number sentence about each picture.
Add **s** to make the name of each kind of cat mean more than one.

_____
+ _____
= _____ tiger _____ .

_____
+ _____
= _____ leopard _____ .

_____
+ _____
= _____ bobcat _____ .

_____
+ _____
= _____ lion _____ .

Disappearing Animals

Cut out the book and put it together.
Write number sentences.
Tell the story in your own words.

8 ___ – ___ = ___

Captain Croc's Zippity Zoo Riverboat by

_____

- - - - - - - - - - - - - - -

_____

Captain Croc 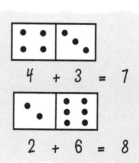 has a riverboat. Animals like to ride in his boat. Here come some now! Turn the page to begin the story.

1

6 ___ + ___ = ___

3 ___ – ___ = ___

Try This!

Make number sentences using dominoes.
You need a set of dominoes, paper, and a pencil.
Look at the number of dots on both halves of a domino. Write a number sentence to show how many dots altogether.

4 + 3 = 7

2 + 6 = 8

Addition and Subtraction Story Problems

Disappearing Animals

2 _____ + _____ = _____

7 _____ − _____ = _____

4 _____ + _____ = _____

5 _____ − _____ = _____

Try This!

1	2	3	4
5	6	7	8
9	10	11	12

Make this game board. You need a large piece of paper, chalk, and coins, buttons, or stones. Use the chalk to make the game board inside on the paper or outside on the sidewalk. Toss two coins or buttons on a paper game board or two stones on a large chalk game board. Subtract the smaller number from the larger number.

Addition and Subtraction Story Problems

Play Like the Animals

Action words tell what people and animals do.
Under each picture, write an action word from the oval.
Then draw lines to match the children with the
animals doing the same actions.

climb dig **slide** jump

1. _____

2. _____

3. _____

4. _____

200   Verbs

Let Me Out!

Some animals hatch from eggs.
Look at these eggs.
Write the name of each animal.

fish   snake

chick   robin

I sing in spring!

1. _____

I love water.

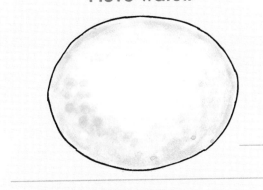

2. _____

I say sssss.

3. _____

I'm yellow.

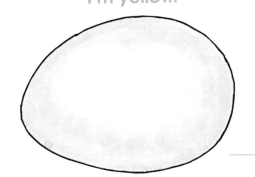

4. _____

Hold the page up to a light or window.
Take a peek inside each egg.
Put a ✓ by the eggs you guessed correctly.

Try This!

Fill a jar with candies, cotton balls, or marbles. Ask family members to guess how many are in the jar. Write down their guesses. Take a guess yourself. Then count the number. Whose guess was closest?

Let Me Out!

Were your guesses correct?
Write the animals you got wrong.

fish   snake
chick   robin

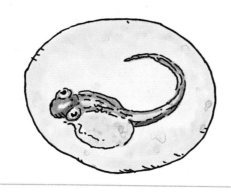

_____

- - - - - - - - - - - -

_____

- - - - - - - - - - - -

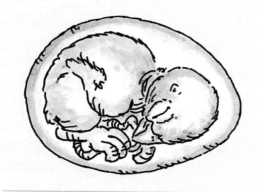

_____

- - - - - - - - - - - -

_____

- - - - - - - - - - - -

Try This!

Animals use many different things to build their nests.
You can build a nest, too. You need twigs, sticks, feathers,
string, grass, and plastic eggs.
1. Weave small sticks and twigs together to make a bowl-shaped nest.
2. Line the nest with soft things like feathers, bits of string, and grass.
3. Put the plastic eggs inside your nest.

Baby Talk

Some baby animals have names that are different from their parents. A baby pig is a **piglet**. What is a baby cat?

Draw a line from each baby to its parent.

calf

lamb

gosling

pup

fawn

cub

Write a baby animal name to finish each sentence.

1. **Seal** goes with _____ .

2. **Tiger** goes with _____ .

Hiding Places

A contraction is two words put together to make one word.
A letter or letters is left out.
An apostrophe (') takes the place of the missing letter or letters.

are not ⟶ are n t ⟶ aren't

Circle the contraction in each sentence.
Then circle the animals in the jungle.

Draw a line from each contraction
to the words that form it.

1. can't	Where is
2. Let's	can not
3. Where's	is not
4. isn't	Let us

What's Happening This Week?

Read the zoo calendar.

Sunday	Monday	Tuesday	Wednesday	Thursday	Friday	Saturday
Sheep Shearing	Birthday Party for Coco the Camel	Storytime Safari	The Zoo Is for You Day! FREE DAY	Jungle Day Walk	Desert Trail Hike	Spring Egg Hunt

Write the day when these things happen.

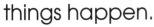

1. _____

2. _____

3. _____

4. _____

Try This!

Make a days of the week journal. You need seven sheets of paper.
1. Write the name of a day on each page. Start with Sunday.
2. Each day, draw a picture or write about something you did.
3. Make a cover for your journal.

Sheep Shearing Today!

Write a number sentence about each picture.

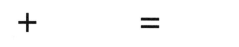

1. _____ + _____ = _____

2. _____ − _____ = _____

3. _____ + _____ = _____

4. _____ − _____ = _____

5. _____ + _____ = _____

6. _____ − _____ = _____

Describe It!

Describing words tell about naming words.

    The **huge** lion roared.

Which word tells about, or **describes**, the lion?

Some describing words tell how animals look or feel.

Write words that tell about the animals.

long   tall   tiny   wet   sleepy   huge

1. _____

2. _____

3. _____

4. _____

5. _____

6. _____

What a Shape!

Draw an alligator.
Follow these steps.

1.

2. Add.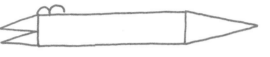

3. Add.

4. Add.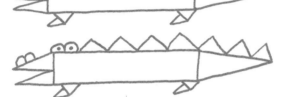

Draw a tiger.
Follow these steps.

1.

2. Add.

3. Add.

4. Add.

1. How many △ s
   in step 4?

2. How many ◯ s
   in step 4?

Think of an animal. Make up a riddle about it. Tell how the animal
looks, feels, and sounds.
Example: I'm thinking of a small bird with a red head. It makes
a rat-tat-tat noise. What is it? (A woodpecker)

Monkey Business

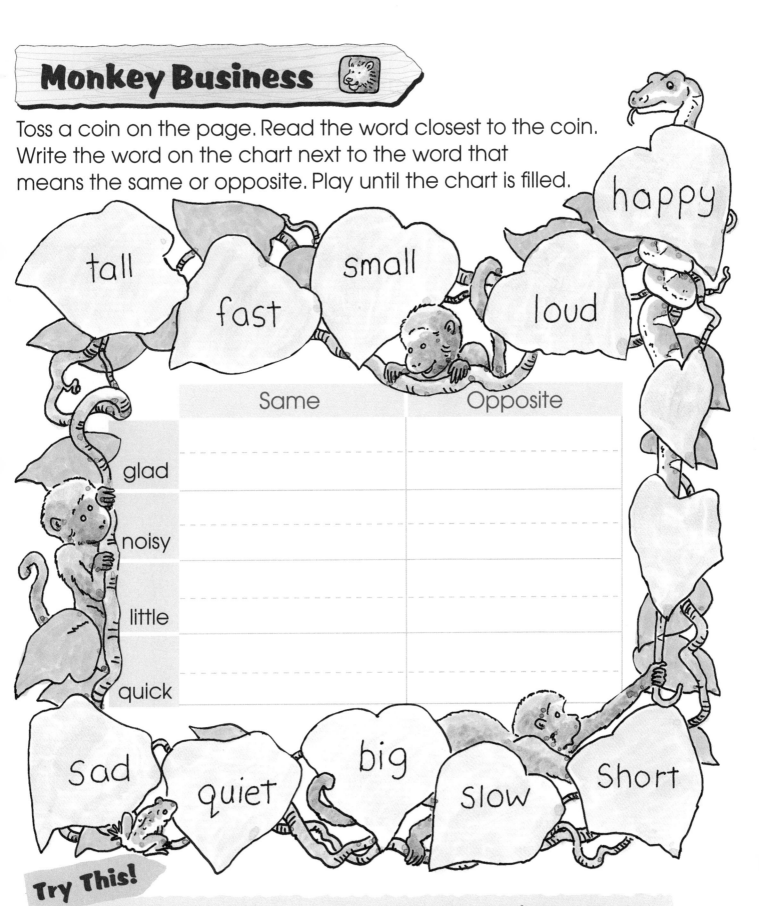

Toss a coin on the page. Read the word closest to the coin. Write the word on the chart next to the word that means the same or opposite. Play until the chart is filled.

tall

fast

small

loud

happy

	Same	Opposite
glad		
noisy		
little		
quick		

sad

quiet

big

slow

Short

Try This!

Copy the words from the leaves on ten cards. Turn the cards facedown to play a game. Turn over two cards at a time. If the words mean the opposite, set the pair aside. If not, turn them facedown again. Play until you have matched all the words.

Big Meets Little

Read the names of the big and little animals.
Add two more names to the chart.

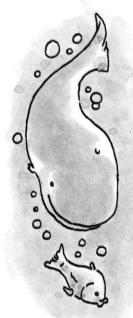

Big Animals	Little Animals
hippo	chipmunk
elephant	butterfly
giraffe	chick

Plan a story about two animals. Write your ideas.

Which big and little animals meet?

_____

_____

Where do they meet?

_____

_____

What is their problem?

_____

_____

How is the problem solved?

_____

_____

Little Weight Watchers

Read the scales.

Color in the boxes to show how many pounds each animal weighs.

	1	2	3	4	5	6	7	8	9	10
tiger cub										
baby porcupine										
fox										
snowy owl										
fawn										
opossum										
weight in pounds	1	2	3	4	5	6	7	8	9	10

In the Seal Pool

You need 15 coins or buttons. Read the chart to find out how many to put in or take out of the pool.

Then count how many are left. Write the numerals in the chart.

Put In	Take Out	How Many Are Left?	Put In	Put In	How Many in All?
9	2		9	6	
10	4		2	8	
12	7		6	5	
8	6		7	7	
15	8		8	6	

Try This!

Use the coins or buttons to write as many different math equations that equal 15 as you can. Then write equations with three numerals that equal 15. Example: 6 + 3 + 6 = 15

Critter's Cafe

Read the clues. Mark the chart with ✓s.
The first one is done for you.

1. Everyone had fruit.
2. Dad and Ben had a taco.
3. Mom had a salad.
4. Anna had a turkey sandwich.
5. Mom, Ben, and Anna had juice.
6. Dad had milk.

	milk	juice	fruit	salad	taco	sandwich
Dad			✓			
Ben			✓			
Mom			✓			
Anna			✓			

Write a person's name under each meal.

1. _____

2. _____

3. _____

4. _____

 Make critter place mats. You need construction paper, crayons or pen,
and clear contact paper. Draw animals on the construction paper.
Cover with clear contact paper.

Zoomobile Tour Game

You need a coin to toss, two buttons for markers, and a sheet of paper and pencil to keep score.

1. Put your button on Start.
2. Toss the coin. If it's heads, move one space.
   If it's tails, move two spaces.
3. Follow the directions on the square on which you land.
   Make a mark on the score sheet for each right answer.
4. The game is over when you reach Finish.
   The most points wins.

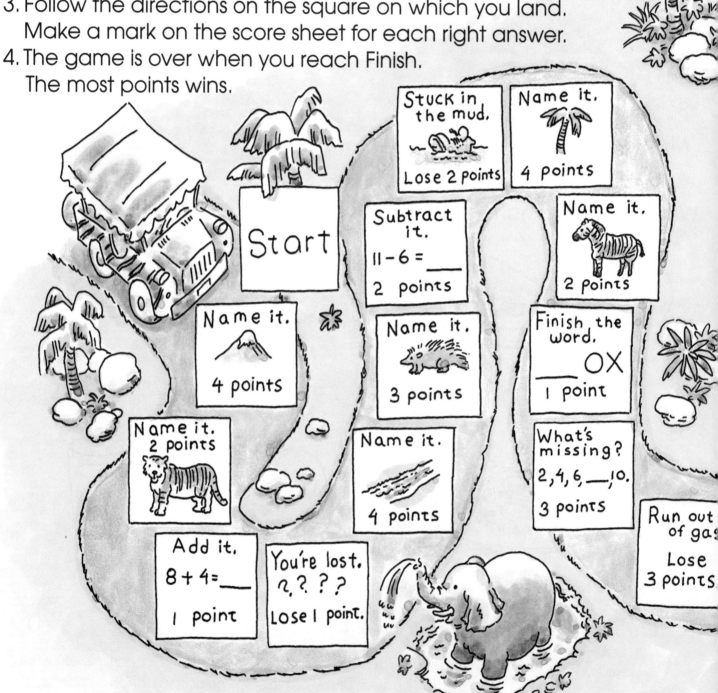

Start

Stuck in the mud.
Lose 2 points

Name it.
4 points

Subtract it.
$11 - 6 =$ ____
2 points

Name it.
2 points

Finish the word.
____ OX
1 point

Name it.
4 points

Name it.
3 points

Name it.
4 points

What's missing?
2, 4, 6, ___, 10.
3 points

Name it.
2 points

Run out of gas
Lose 3 points

Add it.
$8 + 4 =$ ____
1 point

You're lost.
?, ?, ?, ?, ?
Lose 1 point.

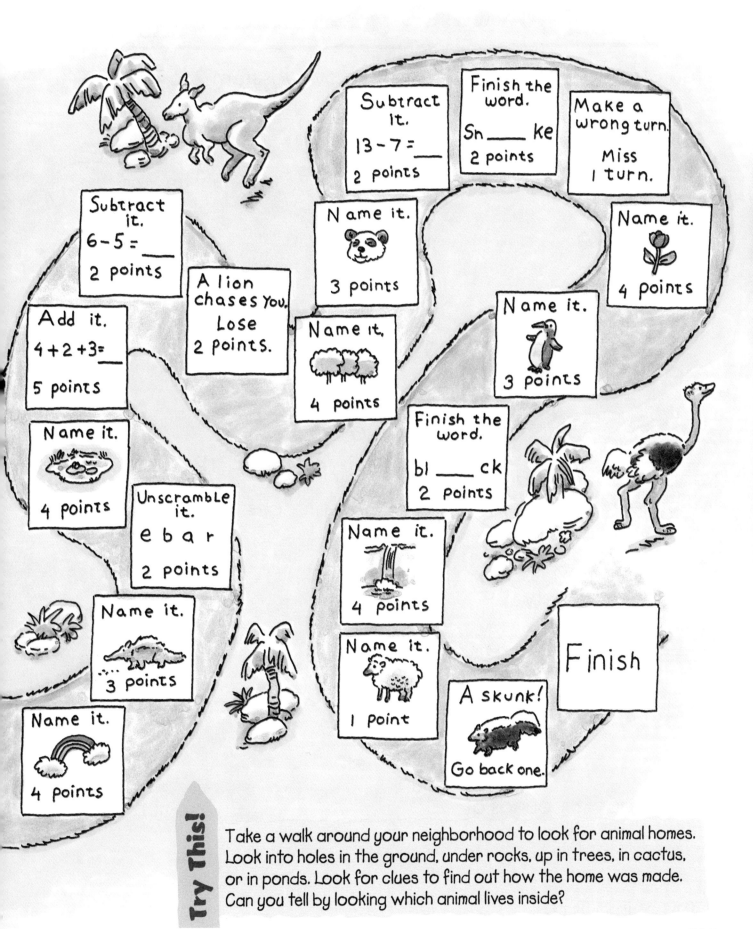

Subtract it.
13 − 7 = ___
2 points

Finish the word.
Sh ___ ke
2 points

Make a wrong turn.
Miss 1 turn.

Subtract it.
6 − 5 = ___
2 points

Name it.
3 points

Name it.
4 points

A lion chases you.
Lose 2 points.

Add it.
4 + 2 + 3 = ___
5 points

Name it.
4 points

Name it.
3 points

Name it.
4 points

Finish the word.
bl ___ ck
2 points

Name it.
4 points

Unscramble it.
e b a r
2 points

Name it.
3 points

Name it.
4 points

Name it.
1 point

A skunk!
Go back one.

Finish

Name it.
4 points

Try This!

Take a walk around your neighborhood to look for animal homes. Look into holes in the ground, under rocks, up in trees, in cactus, or in ponds. Look for clues to find out how the home was made. Can you tell by looking which animal lives inside?

Guess Who's Coming to Dinner

Start at 2. Connect the dots counting by twos from 2 to 40.

•8   •10

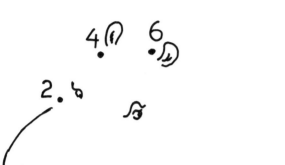 

4   6

2

40   •34   •28   •26   •20   •14   •12

38   36   •32   •30   24   22   18   •16

Read more clues about this animal.
Write the words from the circle in the sentences.

hippo
grass
fat   water

1. This animal is very _____.

2. It spends the day in _____ and eats at night.

3. It can eat 88 pounds of _____ each night.

4. This animal is a _____.

Who Is Lost?

Dad went to buy popcorn. Now he is lost.
Circle the right answers to help him find the family.

1. Where should Dad walk first?

   to the office   to the water fountain   to the zoo entrance

2. Next, Dad should walk to the ___.

   flag   trash can   pond

3. Dad will see the family on the bench if he walks by the ___.

   office   pond   parrot

4. Write **1, 2, 3** to show the right order.

   _____ flag   _____ fountain   _____ parrot

5. Draw a red line on the path Dad should take.

Map Skills/Reading Comprehension

Ape Escape

Help the ape get to the banana tree.
Count by fives from **5** to **50**.
Color the squares with these numbers to show the path.

5	10	6	22	13	8
11	15	7	18	31	14
17	20	25	32	47	71
36	22	30	35	40	48
51	56	43	33	45	50

Try This!

Try counting backwards from 50 to 5.
Then count by twos from 30 to 2. Count
by tens from 100 to 10. How fast can
you count?

Yipes, Stripes!

Look at each row.
Draw the missing picture to fit the pattern.

1.

2.

3.

4. Help the tiger get to her cubs. Find the pattern.
   Color the shapes to finish the path.

Try This!

Collect leaves and flower petals.
Glue them on paper to form
different patterns.

Get Out of Here!

Look at each group of animals.
Circle the one that does not belong.
Then draw an animal that belongs.

Classification

Forest Theater

A telling sentence ends with a period. (.)
An asking sentence ends with a question mark. (?)

Read the sign. Add a (.) or a (?) in the ◯ at the end of each sentence.

Forest Theater

1. The theater is open from 9:00 to 5:00 ◯

2. Have you ever seen an opossum ◯

3. Do you know what a deer eats ◯

4. Come see the show to find out ◯

5. You will meet many forest friends ◯

Declarative and Interrogative Sentences/Punctuation   221

The Big Screen

Write the letters under the numbers.
The first letter is done for you. Then read each animal name.
Draw a line to match the name to the picture.

1	2	3	4	5	6	7	8	9	10	11	12	13	14	15	16
a	b	c	d	e	i	k	l	m	n	o	p	q	r	s	u

The Stars of the Show

1.
11	12	11	15	15	16	9
O						

2.
4	5	5	14

3.
15	7	16	10	7

4.
15	13	16	6	14	14	5	8

Try This!

Finish this riddle about one of the stars of the show. Write your own words. Ask someone to guess your riddle.

This animal lives in the forest.
Its color is _____.
It has _____.
What is it? _____.

Rise and Shine!

When does each animal get up in the morning?
Write the time.

Try This!

Ask someone to use a clock with a second hand to time
you. Guess how many numbers you can write in one minute.
Then do it. How close was your guess?

What do you say to a clock at noon?

¡dn spuɐH

Froggy Grows Up

Look at the pictures.

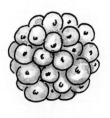     

A   B   C   D   E

Read the sentences.
Write **A, B, C, D,** and **E** to show how Froggy grows up.

1. _____ Froggy is a tiny tadpole.

2. _____ Froggy is a big frog.

3. _____ Froggy is an egg.

4. _____ Froggy grows four legs.

5. _____ Froggy grows two legs.

Animal Poll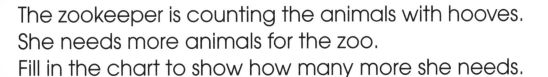

The zookeeper is counting the animals with hooves.
She needs more animals for the zoo.
Fill in the chart to show how many more she needs.

Kinds of Animals		Animals We Want	Animals We Have	How Many More Do We Need?
camel		8	4	
deer		15	9	
giraffe		10	7	
hippo		12	8	
pig		14	7	
sheep		18	9	
buffalo		9	5	
moose		13	6	

Try This! Have you ever seen an old nickel with a picture of a buffalo on it?
You can design your own nickel.
1. Cut a large circle from paper or use a white paper plate.
2. Choose an animal for your coin.
3. Draw what your coin will look like.

Who Is Hiding?

One animal with hooves is very shy.
He is hiding behind these numbers.
Find the sums and differences of the numbers in each row.
Then use the code to find out the animal's name.

7	8	9	10	11	12	13	14	15
r	e	s	m	t	o	f	s	v

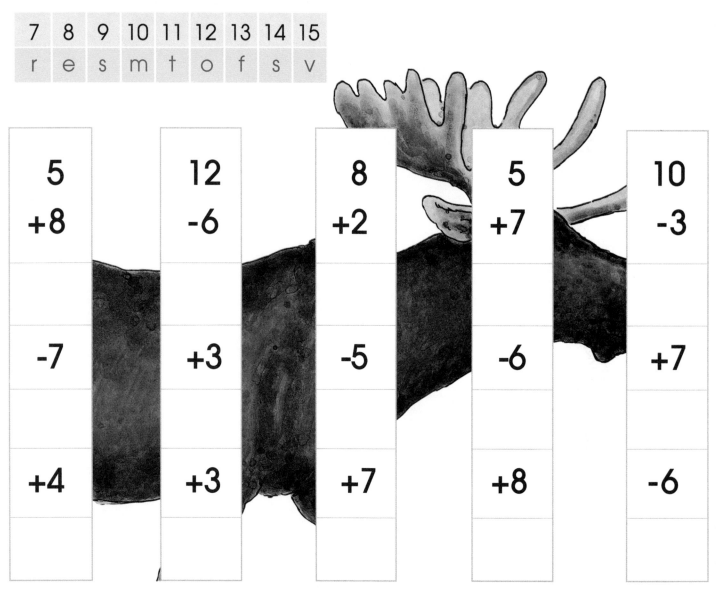

5 +8	12 -6	8 +2	5 +7	10 -3
-7	+3	-5	-6	+7
+4	+3	+7	+8	-6

Look at the last number in each row. Write the letter from
the code box to spell the animal's name.

A Tale of Tracks

Read the story.

Last night we saw some **tracks**. The tracks came from the

forest . They went by the tree . Then they went

down to the pond . We followed the tracks to our

house . What is all that noise? A hungry visitor is eating dinner!

Look at the yard. Follow the tracks.
Number the places from 1 to 4.

Sequence of Events/Reading Comprehension/Animal Behavior

Be a Detective

Look at the story on page 227.
Answer the questions.

1. A fox has four toes on each paw.

   Is the visitor a fox?   Yes   No

2. A deer has hooves.

   Is it a deer?   Yes   No

3. A raccoon has five toes on each paw.

   Is it a raccoon?   Yes   No

4. **What** did you see?

   _____

   -

   _____

5. **Where** did they come from?

   _____

   -

   _____

6. **When** did this happen?

   _____

   -

   _____

Try This!

Look for tracks in your yard.
1. Go outside. Spread some sand on the ground.
2. Place bird seed, nuts, bread, and fruit slices in the center.
3. Stay away for a day. Then check for animal tracks.
4. What do you see? Three toes might mean a bird was there.
   Four front toes and five back toes might mean a squirrel or chipmunk.

Parts of a Whole

A fraction is a part of a whole.

$\dfrac{1}{4}$ → part shaded
→ parts in all

Color the shapes to show the fractions.

$\dfrac{1}{2}$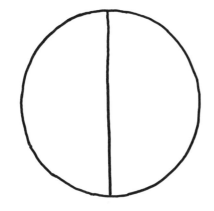

$\dfrac{1}{4}$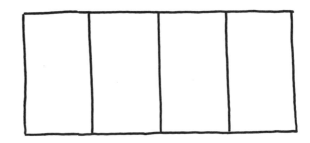

$\dfrac{1}{3}$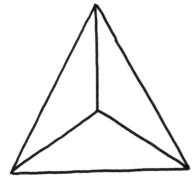

$\dfrac{2}{2}$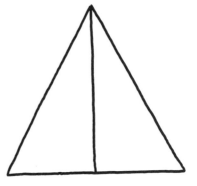

$\dfrac{3}{4}$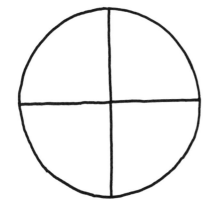

$\dfrac{2}{3}$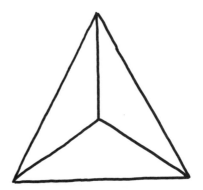

Making Cents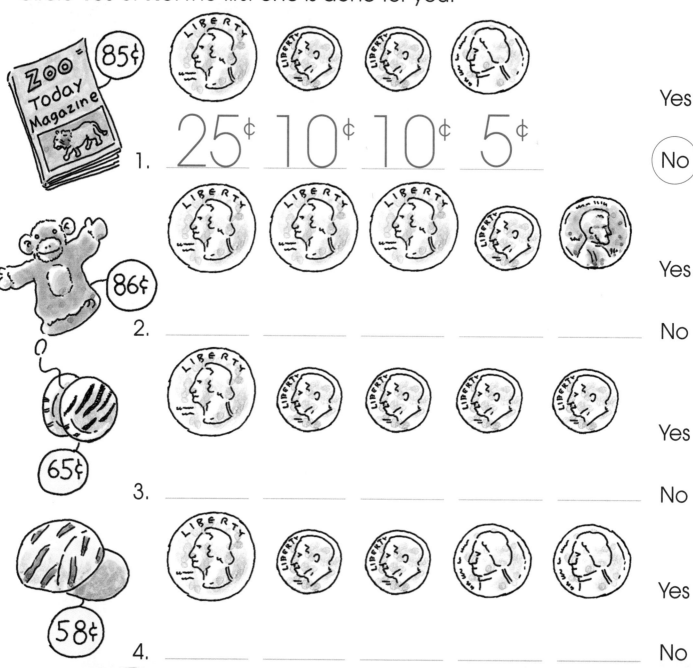

Count the money. Write the amounts on the lines.
Is there enough money to buy the item?
Circle **Yes** or **No**. The first one is done for you.

1. 25¢ 10¢ 10¢ 5¢ _____ Yes (No)

2. _____ Yes No

3. _____ Yes No

4. _____ Yes No

Try This!

Play Yard Sale with some friends. Use self-stick notes to label prices on things around the house. Buy and sell the things you labelled using coins or play money.

Write the price of each item. Then add and write the total.

1.

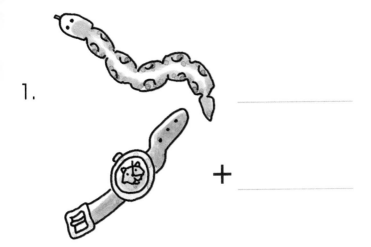

$+$ _____

How much for both? _____

2.

$+$ _____

How much for both? _____

3.

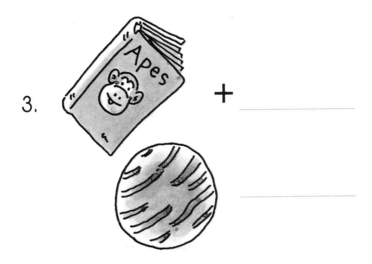

$+$ _____

How much for both? _____

4.

$+$ _____

How much for both? _____

Let's Eat!

What do zoo animals eat? Draw a line from each word to the food.
Color foods in each group to show the fraction.

apples   carrots   bananas   oranges   hay   lettuce

1. $\dfrac{2}{4}$

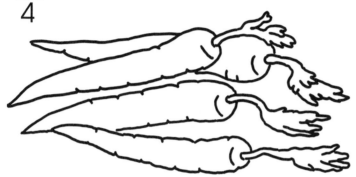

2. $\dfrac{2}{5}$

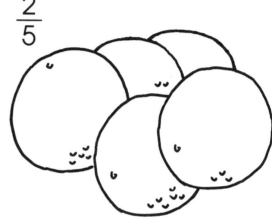

3. $\dfrac{1}{3}$

4. $\dfrac{1}{4}$

5. $\dfrac{2}{3}$

6. $\dfrac{1}{2}$

Butterfly Garden

Take the family through the butterfly garden.
Answer each problem in the space that
follows it. Then circle the hidden butterflies.

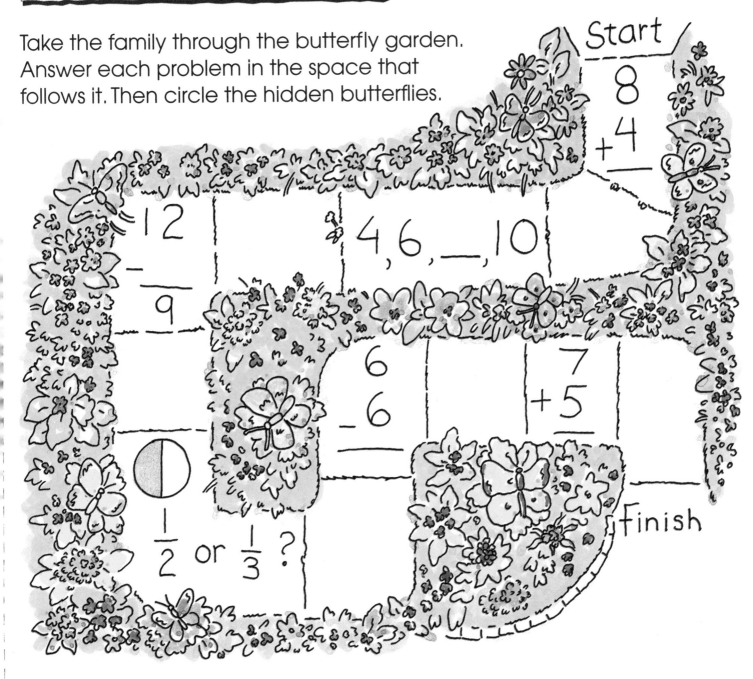

Start

8
+4
___

12
− 9
___

4, 6, __, 10

6
− 6
___

7
+5
___

$\frac{1}{2}$ or $\frac{1}{3}$?

Finish

How many butterflies did you find? _____

Try This!

The right half of a butterfly is the same as
the left half. You need paper, scissors, and
crayons. Fold a sheet of paper in half. Draw
half of a butterfly. Cut out the shape. Then
unfold it. Color both halves the same way.

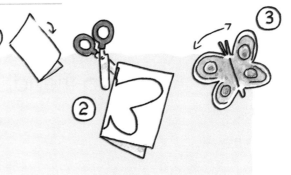

Animal Pen Pal

Pretend you are an animal at a zoo.
Write a letter to the visitors.
Remember to sign your name as the animal.

Month → Day → Year →

Date

Dear Visitors, Greeting

Body

Closing ⟶ Your zoo friend,

Signature ⟶

Animal Count

In this picture are some of the animals
you met in this book.
Guess how many there are.

Now count the animals.
Watch out!
Some animals are hiding.
How close was your guess?

A Tale of a Tail

A bear's tail is short and stubby.
One Native American tale explains why.

Once, bears  had **long, furry tails**. Then something

happened. Bear  was hungry for crayfish  .

But the pond was frozen. So Bear asked

Fox  for help. Tricky Fox told Bear

to make a hole in the ice. He told Bear  to hang his long

tail through the hole. When a crayfish  pinched it, he

could pull the crayfish 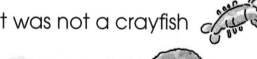 up. Bear  felt a

pinch. But it it was not a crayfish  . His tail was frozen into

the pond . Bear pulled so hard that his tail

broke off. Bears  have had **short tails** ever since.

Try This!

Write your own tale. Think of an animal and what
is special about it. Tell how it got to be that way.
Draw pictures to go with your story.

Reading for Details and Cause & Effect Relationships

1. What kind of tails did bears once have?

_____

- -

_____

2. What kind of tails do bears have now?

_____

- -

_____

3. Why did bears' tails change?

_____

- -

_____

_____

- -

Compare the Bears!

Black Bears: 4-5 feet long; 150-400 pounds
Grizzly Bears: 6-7 1/2 feet long; 300-900 pounds
Polar Bears: 6-8 feet long, up to 1,500 pounds
Coastal Brown Bears: 6-8 1/2 feet long; up to 1,600 pounds

Grizzly Bear

Brown Bear

Black Bear

Polar Bear

There are many reasons people like zoos.
Write some of your reasons here to finish this poem.

Zoos

I like zoos.
I'll tell you why.

Because, _____

_____

Because, _____

_____

Because, _____

_____

Because! That's why!
I like zoos.

Try This!

Make an animal puppet to help you say your poem.
You need a paper bag, construction paper, scissors,
glue, crayons, and markers. Draw a face on the flap
at the bottom of the bag.
1. Cut out and add ears.
2. Add a mouth and feet, paws, or wings.
3. Put your hand inside the bag. Move the flap up and
   down to make your puppet talk.

Activities to Share: Language Arts

Here is a list of excellent animal books to look for in your local library or bookstore. The list includes fiction and nonfiction.

- *Crocodile Smile* by Sara Weeks, illustrated by Lois Ehlert. HarperCollins, 1994. Bright picture collages enhance this book of animal songs and poems. The book comes with a cassette tape.

- *From Head to Toe* by Eric Carle. HarperCollins, 1997. A variety of familiar animals invites the reader to copy their antics as they wiggle, stomp, thump, and bend across the pages of this book.

- *The Great Kapok Tree: A Tale of the Amazon Rain Forest* by Lynne Cherry. Gulliver Books, Harcourt, 1990. The great kapok tree is in danger of being cut down. What will happen to all the forest creatures if this occurs?

- *A Hippopotamusn't and Other Animal Poems* by J. Patrick Lewis. Dial Books, 1990. This is a collection of funny verse about all kinds of animals. The humorous illustrations add to the fun.

- *How the Guinea Fowl Got Her Spots: An African Tale* retold and illustrated by Barbara Knutson. Carolrhoda, 1990. When Guinea Fowl helps her friend escape from a lion, she is rewarded with a disguise that will camouflage her.

- *How the Ostrich Got Its Long Neck: A Tale from the Akamba of Kenya* retold by Verna Aardema. Scholastic, 1995. At one time Ostrich had a short neck. That changed after an encounter with a crocodile.

- *In the Small, Small Pond* by Denise Fleming. Henry Holt, 1993. Spring has sprung, and a bright green frog leaps out of the grass and into the pond where a host of other animals make their homes. The reader follows tadpoles, minnows, turtles, dragonflies, and ducks through spring, summer, and autumn. When winter arrives, the frog burrows deep into the pond to wait for spring's return.

- *Little Elephant* by Miela Ford with photographs by Tana Hoban. Greenwillow Books, 1994. Captioned photographs depict a young elephant's adventures playing in the water before returning to the safety of its mother.

- *Penguin Pete and Little Tim* by Marcus Pfister. North-South Books, 1994. Penguin Pete is a proud father who cannot wait to show his son the wonders of their chilly world.

- *Splash, Splash* by Jeff Sheppard. MacMillan, 1994. When a group of animals unexpectedly goes for a swim, each reaction is very different. The many animal sound words make this a great read-aloud.

- *Time to Sleep* by Denise Fleming. Henry Holt, 1997. The chill in the air tells Bear that it's time for her winter-long nap. She must tell Snail, who tells Skunk, who tells Turtle. Each puts off going to sleep in order to see, smell, hear, and taste the signs of the season.

V for Vanishing: An Alphabet of Endangered Animals by Patricia Mullins. HarperCollins, 1994. Beautiful collages depict many animals that are in danger of extinction.

Here are two videos about animals.

The Animal Show Starring Stinky and Jake. Polygram Home Video. Muppets Jake and Stinky host a talk show with wild animal guests.

Really Wild Animals: Swingin' Safari. National Geographic Kids. A globe named Spin is the host on a journey to Africa. You will see how zebras, elephants, lions, and other animals grow, play, and hunt for food and learn about the climatic conditions of Africa. Others in the series: *Totally Tropical Rain Forest* and *Wonders Down Under.*

Social Studies

There are many things your family can do to help preserve the environment and help save endangered animals. Here are some suggestions.

In Your Home

Recycle everything you can: newspapers, glass, cans, aluminum, motor oil, scrap metal.

Save kitchen scraps for a compost pile.

Use phosphate-free dish and laundry soaps.

Avoid using pesticides.

Use cold water in the washer whenever possible.

Use cloth napkins and washable rags.

Reuse brown paper and plastic bags.

Use reusable plastic storage containers rather than foil or plastic wrap.

Turn down the heat one degree for each hour you are away from home or asleep.

Turn off lights and the television when you are not in the room.

Feed the birds; make birdhouses and bird baths.

Compost leaves and yard debris.

When Shopping

Don't buy foods in plastic containers if there is an alternative.

Avoid disposable items. If you must buy disposables, buy paper rather than plastics.

Put parcels in one large sack rather than many small bags.

Buy in bulk and buy locally grown products.

Science

- Some experts claim that there has been a 50% reduction in the population of song-birds over the past century. Do some simple projects with your child to house and feed some feathered friends. The world's easiest birdhouse to make uses a 6" to 8" green-and-orange gourd. Drill or whittle an opening for the bird. Scrape out the seeds. Drill or whittle a 1/2" drain hole at the bottom and a 1/4" hole through the top to insert a line for hanging. This house will last for one season.

- To feed the birds, sew a garland of popcorn, grain cereals, and dried fruits to hang in trees. Or smear peanut butter on pine cones and sprinkle with seeds. Remember to place these where greedy squirrels might not be able to get to them.

- Squirrels, however, are very clever and can hang upside down to feed. One idea is to leave an ear of corn out for the squirrels so they won't bother the birds' food.

- Have you ever seen squirrels busily burying nuts in the fall? How do they know where to find them later? Squirrels do remember the general area in which they buried nuts, but they rely on their sense of smell to locate buried nuts. Count out 20 unshelled peanuts. Have your child put them in secret hiding places around the house. You may want to keep a list of the places. Wait two days. Then have your child search for the nuts. How many nuts did he or she find? How did your child find them?

Math

Take math into the kitchen where you and your child can make animal-theme foods for a snack or meal. Here are two suggestions.

- Hippo-Hip Hooray Salad
  For each salad: one lettuce leaf, one pear half, cheese triangles, 2 raisins, 2 cherries

  1. Place a lettuce leaf on a plate.
  2. Top with a pear half, placing the sliced side down.
  3. Add cheese triangle ears, raisin eyes, and cherry nose.
     Make one salad for each family member.

- A Hoot of a Treat
  For each treat: one slice of wheat bread, tuna or chicken salad,
  2 slices of egg and black olives, 1 triangle of cheese, pine nuts

  1. Cut the bread on one end to form owl's head.
  2. Cover the bread with a favorite spread.
  3. Place 2 egg slices with black olive slices for eyes.
  4. Add a cheese beak and pine nuts for claws. Enjoy!

Summer Fun

Dani and Josh live on Shady Lane.
Three friends live there, too.

School is out! Summer fun begins!
Circle the friends' names in the puzzle.

```
S  T  W  E  N  W
B  I  L  L  Y  T
L  P  E  D  R  O
K  C  D  A  N  I
G  J  O  S  H  J
```

HOT IDEA

Make a word puzzle using the names of friends. Ask one friend to solve the puzzle.

Draw a picture of your favorite summertime activity.

Follow the Friends

What does each friend like to do in the summer?
Write a letter from the box to finish each word.

b	h	s	c	f	r

_____ _____

_____ wim

_____ amp

_____ ish

_____ ide

_____ ike

_____ aseball

HOT idea

Think of things you can do with a group of friends. Try to put on a magic show, go star gazing, plant a garden, or have a garage sale.

What do you like to do?

_____

_____

Here Comes Summer!

What things go with summer?
Draw a line from each picture to the sun.

beach
towel

baseball cap

mittens

shorts

boots

suitcase

watermelon

beach ball

picnic

swimsuit

snowman

HOT IDEA

Write a summer poem:
Bright hot sun.
Campers having fun.
Swimmers on the go.
NO cold snow!

It is time for baseball practice. Dani and Josh run outside.
Read the sentences. Write each friend's name by his or her house.

Dani and Josh

Billy has a flower garden.   His house is blue.

Pedro has a pond.   His house is red.

Wen has a fence.   Her house is yellow.

To Baseball Field →

Go Team!

The five friends play for the Rockets.
Write the team number on each child's
team shirt.

Dani is number **six**.
Josh is number **one**.
Pedro is number **three**.
Billy is number **eight**.
Wen is number **seven**.

There are **9** players on a baseball team.
How many more players are needed to play a game? _____

COOL FACT

The Baseball Hall of Fame
is in Cooperstown, New York.

Batter Up!

Read what each friend says.
Write their names in order.

Batting Order

1.

2.

3.

4.

5.

Keeping Score

The Rockets played their first game with the Flyers. Add to fill in the missing numbers.

INNING	Rockets	Flyers	TOTAL RUNS
1	1		3
2	2	2	4
3	1		1
4		0	2
5		3	5
6	1		2
7			
8			
9			
TOTAL			17

How many innings did they play? _____

_____

Who won the game? _____

Team Treat!

After the game, the Rockets were hungry.
Circle the coins needed to buy each item.
Use the fewest coins you can.

 Quarter = 25¢   Dime = 10¢   Nickel = 5¢   Penny = 1¢

1.

2.

3.

4.

Splash City

The water park opens today!
From 1–6, number the names in ABC order.

WELCOME TO SPLASH CITY

Slippery Slide

Paddleboats

Wave Pool

Log Ride

Tube Trails

Beach

HOT IDEA

Play a game of water volleyball. Use a water balloon instead of a ball.

What would be your favorite ride?

_____

_____

Slippery Slide Ride

Help Wen get down the water slide.
Circle word pairs that rhyme.
Then draw a line to connect the word pairs.

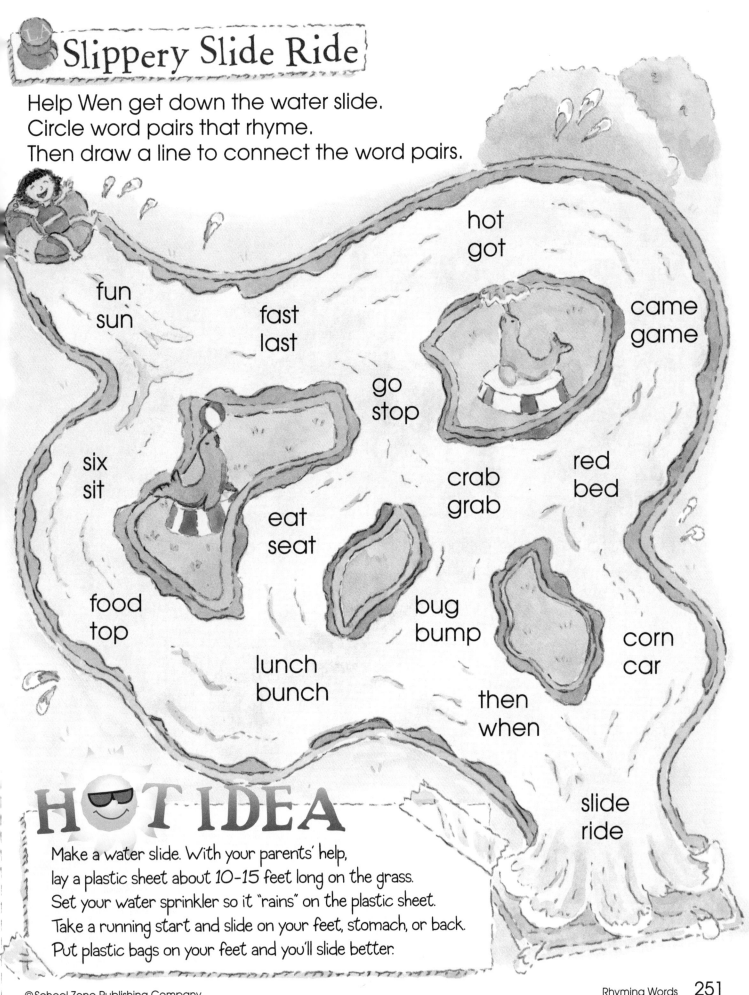

hot
got

fun
sun

fast
last

came
game

six
sit

go
stop

red
bed

crab
grab

eat
seat

food
top

bug
bump

corn
car

lunch
bunch

then
when

slide
ride

H☉T IDEA

Make a water slide. With your parents' help,
lay a plastic sheet about 10-15 feet long on the grass.
Set your water sprinkler so it "rains" on the plastic sheet.
Take a running start and slide on your feet, stomach, or back.
Put plastic bags on your feet and you'll slide better.

Ride the Waves

Read each word in the wave pool.

Write a word from the pool that means the opposite.

_____   _____

1. out _____   2. warm _____

3. little _____   4. quiet _____

5. slow _____

6. sad _____

Draw yourself in the wave pool with a friend.

HOT IDEA

Play baseball in your yard. In place of a ball use a water balloon.

That's Not Right!

Look at the wave pool. What's not right?
Circle up to 8 things that don't look right.

NO RUNNING

Write one pool rule.

_____

_____

H☀T IDEA

You don't want to get too much sun on a hot summer day. Make a sun hat for yourself.
You will need a piece of newspaper (two pages with a fold down the middle).

1. Fold the outer edge down to make a point at the top center.

2. Fold the bottom flap up to meet the bottom of the triangle.

3. Then fold it over again.

4. Do the same on the other side.

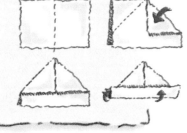

Off to the Dude Ranch

Pedro and his family are spending a week at Circle S Ranch. Answer the questions to help them get to the riding stables.

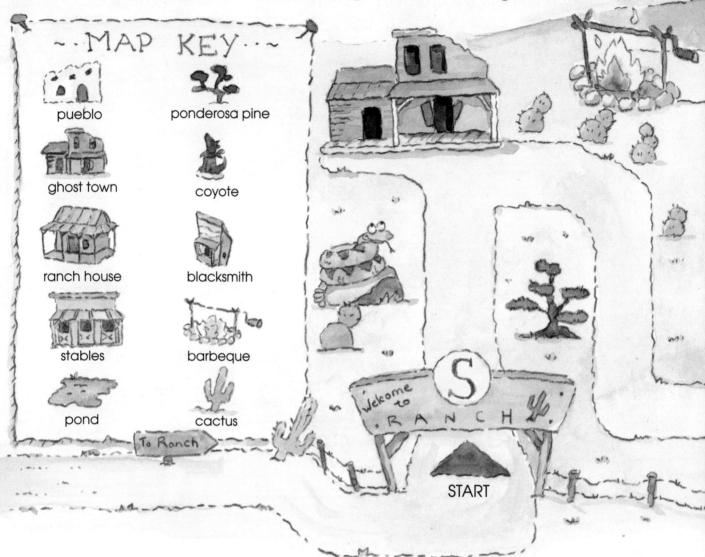

1. What will they pass first?   ghost town   cows

2. Will they turn at the ranch house?   yes   no

3. Will they cross over a bridge?   yes   no

4. What will they pass after the bridge?   coyote   pueblo

5. What is the last thing they will pass?   barbeque pit   pond

Draw a line to show the path.

What two things would you
like to see at Circle S Ranch?

_____

_____

_____

_____

COOL FACT

If you want to visit a ghost
town, go to New Mexico.
There are more than 130
ghost towns in this state!

Giddyup!

Draw a line between two horses that make a compound word.

sun

top

after

down

down

hill

noon

tree

HOT IDEA

Whether you are riding or walking the trail, make a nutty mix to take along for a snack. Chop up favorite candy or granola bars. Add corn nuts, mixed nuts, bite-size crackers, dry fruits, and cereal. YUM!

Saving for Souvenirs

Josh and Dani saved money for a family trip.
Count the money each one has.
Write the amounts on the lines.

Quarters

_____ ¢

Quarters

_____ ¢

Dimes

_____ ¢

Dimes

_____ ¢

Nickels

_____ ¢

Nickels

_____ ¢

Pennies

_____ ¢

Pennies

_____ ¢

Josh's Total: _____ ¢

Dani's Total: _____ ¢

HOT IDEA

To make a great souvenir of your summer travels, take along a cap and a permanent marker. Ask new friends you meet along the way to sign your cap.

Who saved more?

_____

- - - - - - - - - - - - - - - - - - -

_____

Camping Out!

Dani and Josh went on a family camping trip.
Use the map to answer the questions.

1. A camper is by the playground.   yes   no

2. There is a path to the lake.   yes   no

3. The hiking trail is near the camp store.   yes   no

4. Tents and campers are in the same area.   yes   no

5. The picnic area is near the tree fort.   yes   no

6. A bath house is by the lake.   yes   no

Wen's family took a trip to the beach.
Name the beach things Wen sees.
Color the pictures to finish the patterns.

Draw and color the pictures to finish the patterns.

_____

_____

GiGGLES

Knock, knock!
Who's there?
Shell.
Shell who?
She'll be coming 'round the
mountain when she comes!

_____

On the Beach

Wen and her family saw many things at the beach. Write the name of each thing on the chart.

OKAY FOR SWIMMING

flag

kite

boat

lifeguard

seagulls

crab

shells

COOL FACT

Hermit crabs don't make their own shells. They find a shell that fits and move in. If they don't, they might be eaten by a gull!

Living Things	Non-Living Things

Dig In!

Wen and her brother like to build sand castles.
Write the numerals 1–5 to tell the order in which things happen.

GiGGLES

Why is the beach
so noisy?

Because waves are always
breaking on it!

As a Matter of Fact

Read each animal fact. Use the vowel code to write the animal name. Write the sentence number in the box next to the animal it describes.

a	e	i	o	u
●	▲	★	◆	■

1. I have eight arms and large eyes.

◆ c t ◆ p ■ s _____

2. I blow myself up when I am scared.

b l ◆ w f ★ s h _____

3. I have a soft body, so I find a shell to live in.

h ▲ r m ★ t c r ● b _____

4. I have sharp teeth on my snout.

s ● w f ★ s h _____

5. I talk with whistles, chirps, and other sounds.

d ◆ l p h ★ n _____

COOL FACT

Starfish do not have a brain.

Travel Tips

Help Billy's family plan a trip. Read about different places.
Write the missing word from the box.

SPEND THE NIGHT

In Coyote

_____

Camping Is Great

In
Black Bear

_____

Turtle

_____

A great place to visit!

Climb

GIANT

_____

Different Places

Fill in the missing word to complete each sentence.
Use the words in the box to help you.

water	dry
cold	hot
trees	

_____

1. It's very _____ high in the mountains.

   _____

2. Deserts are _____ during the day.

   _____

3. The sand is _____ from lack of rain.

   _____

4. Islands are surrounded by _____ .

   _____

5. Forests are lands with _____ .

GiGGLES

How is an island
like the letter t?

Both are in the middle
of water.

Where does Billy's family go?
Unscramble the letters and write the words: **t o y o e C   e s D r t e**

_____

Getting There

Summer is a good time to travel. People go from place to place across the country. What different kinds of transportation do they use?

Read each rhyme. Then write the name of the transportation it describes.

1. I rhyme with hike. _____

2. I rhyme with us. _____

3. I rhyme with star. _____

4. I rhyme with pet. _____

5. I rhyme with plane. _____

Travel Shapes

Follow the directions to draw a jet and a ship.

1. Draw an oval.

2. Add five triangles.

3. Draw squares for windows. Add some clouds.

Where would you like a jet to take you?

_____

1. Draw five rectangles.

2. Add two triangles.

3. Draw ten circles. Add some waves.

Where would you like a ship to take you?

_____

Wish You Were Here!

Read each postcard. Draw a line to match the card with the friend who wrote it. Write the friend's name on the card.

Howdy,
   This ranch is lots of fun. I ride a horse named Sugarlump. I learned to rope a calf. Tonight there is a cookout.

_____

_____

Hi,
   We are having a great time camping. We saw deer and a bear yesterday. Wish you were here.

_____

_____

_____

_____

Write words from the box to answer the questions.

ocean   calf   bear   **horse**   desert

_____

_____

1. Dani and Josh saw what animal? _____

_____

2. Where did Wen swim? _____

Hi,
   The desert is neat. One cactus is taller than my house! I heard a coyote last night. See you soon.

_____

_____

_____

Hi,
   The ocean is great! I swim every day. I have made three sandcastles. Wish you were here to look for seashells.

_____

_____

_____

SUGARLUMP

HOT IDEA

If you could build a bridge from your house to anywhere in the world, where would it be? Why?

_____

3. What animal did Pedro rope? _____

_____

4. Who is Sugarlump? _____

_____

5. Where does a cactus grow? _____

Gone Fishing

The five friends were home from their trips.
They went fishing. Read the picture graph.
Write the number of fish each one caught.

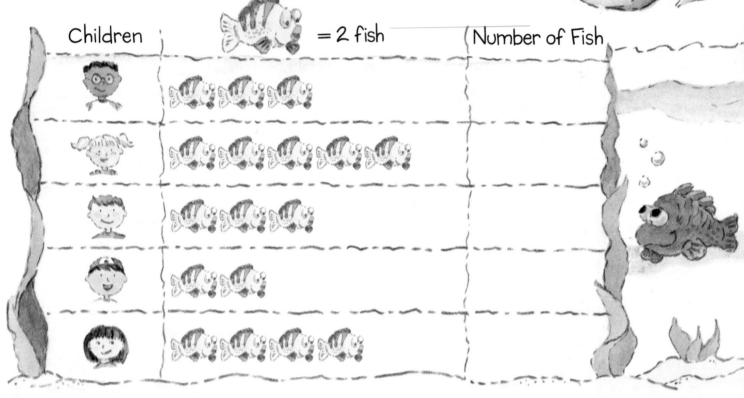

Children	= 2 fish	Number of Fish

1. Who caught the most fish?

2. Who caught the fewest fish?

3. Who caught the same number of fish?

GiGGLES

What's the difference
between a piano and a fish?

You can tune a piano, but you
can't tuna fish!

Fish Tales

Dad's fish is 4 pennies long.

Estimate how many pennies long each fish is.
Now measure with pennies.
How close was your guess?

Estimate	Measure

COOL FACT

When a fish called a flounder hatches, it has one eye on each side of its head. After living on the bottom of the sea, one eye twists around so that both eyes are on one side of the flounder's head.

Nature Spy

Josh and Wen are looking for insects. Not all bugs are insects.

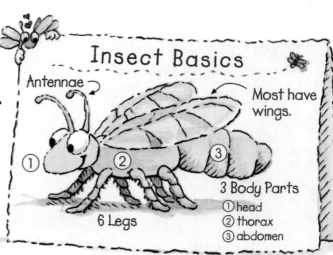

Insect Basics

Antennae

Most have wings.

① ② ③

6 Legs

3 Body Parts
① head
② thorax
③ abdomen

Check the boxes next to the bugs that are insects.

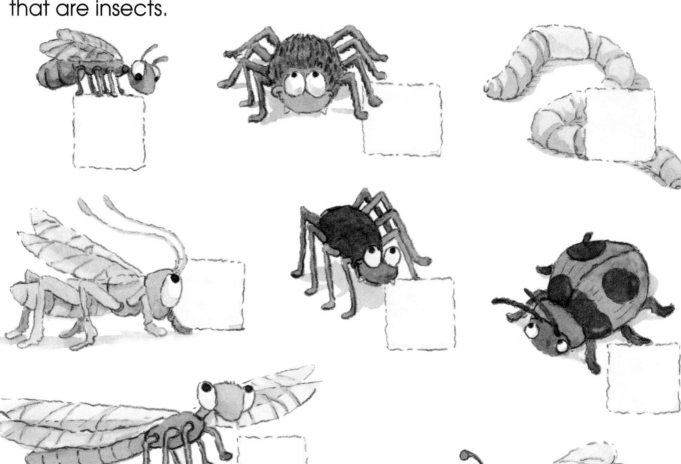

COOL FACT

A click beetle has a special talent. If it is on its back, it will slowly bend in the middle and pop straight up into the air with a loud "click!"

Buggy Backyard

Josh and Wen decided to be detectives for the day.
Look at the picture. Circle the hidden insects.

How many insects did you find?

Go outside. Look at an insect with a magnifying glass.
Draw what you see.

COOL FACT

The firebrat really is a "brat" if it gets into your home. It likes to eat wallpaper paste, crackers, and clothes! The whirligig beetle twirls around in a pond making zigzag patterns.

Rub-a-Dub-Dub

Josh and Dani planned a neighborhood dog wash.
Read the sentences. Draw a line to show where they go.

1. First, they go to Mrs. Green's.
2. Next, they go to Mr. Berry's.
3. Then, they go to the Ride house.
4. Last, they go to Mrs. Ball's.

HOT IDEA

Write a rhyme about washing a dog. Use rhyming words such as rub, dub, tub, and scrub.

Rub-a-dub-dub,
Washing dogs in a tub.
Rub-a-dub-dub,
How many dogs did they scrub? _____ dogs

What's Happening?

This calendar tells what is happening where the friends live.

Sunday	Monday	Tuesday	Wednesday	Thursday	Friday	Saturday
Berry picking at Eno Farm	Farmers' Market opens today!	Berry Baking Contest	4th of July Parade 11:00	Fireworks at the lake 9:00	County Fair today through Saturday	Blue Ribbon Day at the Fair

Write the day when these things happen.

1.

2.

3.

4.

June Weather

This is a picture graph about the weather in June.

sunny	☀	☀	☀	☀	☀	☀	☀	☀	☀	☀
rainy	💧	💧	💧	💧	💧	💧	💧			
cloudy	☁	☁	☁	☁	☁	☁				

0   1   2   3   4   5   6   7   8   9   10
Number of Days

1. On how many days did the people need an ☂ ? _____

   Why? _____

2. On how many days would you wear 🕶 ? _____

   Why? _____

3. What kind of weather happened least during June?

   _____

   _____

   _____

Bonus !

4. What month comes after June? _____

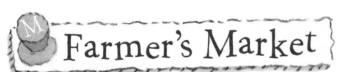

Farmer's Market

Write each sum. Color the picture.

1. 8 + 3 = _____

2. 11 − 3 = _____

3. 6 + 6 = _____

4. 12 − 6 = _____

5. 5 + 4 = _____

6. 9 − 4 = _____

HOT IDEA

Make math flash cards you can solve and eat! Spread peanut butter on graham crackers. Use licorice whips to form a number problem. Solve the problem and eat!

One Potato, Two Potatoes

Write the food names in ABC order.
Write the numeral to tell how many.

potatoes

carrots

apples

melons

lettuce

bananas

Food in ABC Order	How many?

HOT IDEA

Count the numbers of fruits and vegetables again. This time count backwards! 3-2-1 melons!

Graph It!

Fill in the graph. Color one box for each fruit and vegetable on page 278.

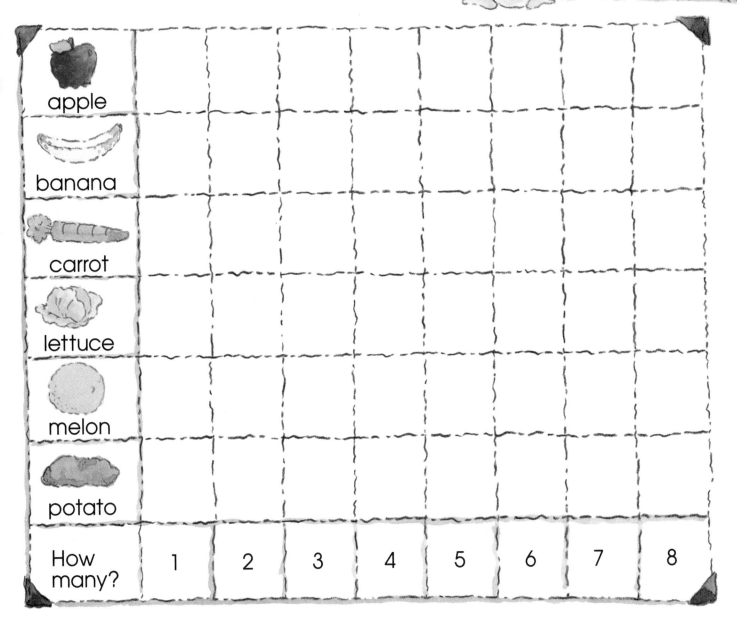

	1	2	3	4	5	6	7	8
apple								
banana								
carrot								
lettuce								
melon								
potato								
How many?	1	2	3	4	5	6	7	8

Circle the correct answer.

1. Are there more apples or potatoes?

2. Are there more melons or heads of lettuce?

3. Are there fewer carrots or bananas?

4. Are there fewer apples or carrots?

How Many?

The friends saw many kinds of fruits and vegetables.
Write how many of each.

1. _____ tens   _____ ones

How many? _____

2. _____ tens   _____ ones

How many? _____

3. _____ tens   _____ ones

How many? _____

4. _____ tens   _____ ones

How many? _____

5. _____ tens   _____ ones

How many? _____

6. _____ tens   _____ ones

How many? _____

How many tens? How many ones?

	tens	ones
40		
36		

Bunches of Berries

Billy and Pedro went berry picking.
Pedro made piles of 5 berries. Count by fives.
Write the numbers.

5
___

How many did Pedro pick?_____

Billy made piles of 10 berries. Count by tens.
Write the numbers.

10
___

How many did Billy pick?_____

HOT IDEA

Juicy Painting
Mash blueberries through a sieve. Use the juice to
paint a picture. What color is the juice?

Berry Good Muffins

Billy and Pedro made blueberry muffins for their friends.
Read what they did. Number the steps 1–4.

Bake until golden brown.

First, mix the batter.

Next, add the blueberries.

Then, pour into muffin cups.

H T IDEA

Make Your Own Blueberry Muffins   *Parent-Supervised Activity!

You need:

1 3/4 cups flour	1/2 tsp salt	2 eggs
1/3 cup sugar	1/4 cup cooking oil	1 tsp vanilla
2 tsps baking powder	3/4 cup milk	1 cup blueberries

1. Heat oven to 400°. Put 12 paper baking cups in muffin tin.
2. Combine the dry ingredients.
3. Mix the oil, milk, eggs, and vanilla together.
4. Add wet mixture to dry ingredients. Stir in berries.
5. Pour into muffin cups.
6. Bake 20-25 minutes or until golden brown. YUM!

Hooray for the Red, White, and Blue

Each year on July 4, we celebrate our country's birthday.
This day is called Independence Day. It began in 1776.

A sentence has a **naming part**.
The naming part tells who or what the sentence is about.
Write the naming part of each sentence.

1. The parade begins at 2:00 P.M.   parade

2. Pedro will carry the flag.

3. Drums will be played.

4. Bells will ring.

5. Our town loves a parade.

Read the invitation.

COME TO A PARTY!

What: 4th of July picnic

When: July 4 at 2:00 P.M.

Where: 123 Shady Lane

Who: Wen Chu

Bring your favorite picnic food.

Circle the answer to each question.

1. Who is having a party?	Billy	Wen
2. What is the party for?	holiday	birthday
3. What day is the party?	June 5	July 4
4. What time is the party?	2:00 P.M.	12:00 P.M.
5. Where will the party be?	123 Shady Lane	Billy's house

What picnic food will you bring to the party?

_____

_____

_____

GiGGLES

Where can a burger get a great night's sleep?

On a bed of lettuce

©School Zone Publishing Company

Backyard Barbeque

A sentence has a **telling part**.
The telling part tells what someone or something does.

Underline the telling part of each sentence.

1. Dani <u>brings milk</u>.

2. Josh has bananas.

3. Wen takes a salad.

4. Billy carries hot dogs.

5. They all eat together.

Write a sentence about a picnic.
Underline the telling part.

_____

_____

_____

Who didn't bring anything?_____

Ka-Boom!

What are the friends saying about the fireworks?
Use words from the box to write each contraction.

Isn't   Don't   We're   Let's   I'm

_____
- - - - - - - - - -
_____ watch!
Let us

_____
- - - - - - - - - -
_____ this great?
Is not

_____
- - - - - - - - - -
_____ blink!
Do not

_____
- - - - - - - - - -
_____ lucky!
We are

_____
- - - - - - - - - -
_____ watching!
I am

H☀T IDEA

Make a Fourth of July Spinner

You need string, scissors, crepe paper, and a spring clothespin.

1. Cut a piece of string as long as your arm.
2. Thread the string through the hole in the clothespin and tie a knot.
3. Cut crepe paper strips as tall as you.
4. Clip the clothespin to one end of the strips.
5. Hold the end of the string and wave your arm to twirl the strips.

Write the time next to each clock.
Draw a line to match the clock to what happens.

1. _____ o'clock

2. _____ o'clock

3. _____ o'clock

4. _____ o'clock

5. _____ o'clock

County Fair!

What is the most popular event at the fair?
Color one box for each person.

1. How many are at the tractor pull? _____

2. How many are at the roping contest? _____

3. What event had the most people? _____

4. What event had the fewest people? _____

What a Ride!

Write the time.

1.

half past _____

_____ : _____

2.

half past _____

_____ : _____

3.

half past _____

_____ : _____

Draw hands to show the time.

4. 8:00

5. 11:30

6. 3:00

7. 4:30

GiGGLES

What goes up but never comes down?

Your age!

How Much?

Fill in the number of coins Billy needs to have the correct amount.

Clyde's Carnival Treasures

	Quarter	Dime	Nickel	Penny
😊 8¢	0	0	1	3
🍦 15¢				
🍭 20¢				
🎟️ 46¢				
🧢 39¢				
🧸 58¢				

H🌞T IDEA

Set up a "pretend" auction with your friends. Collect items that will go up for bid. You be the first auctioneer and have your friends make bids on an object. The highest bidder counts out the correct amount of "play money" to pay. The highest bidder then becomes auctioneer and the bidding begins on a new item.

Animals at the Fair

Write the naming word for the animals at the fair. Use the words in the box if you need to.

pig   horse
dog   duck
cow   goat

1. The _____ is tall.

2. A _____ is fat!

3. The _____ has horns.

4. A spotted _____ moos.

5. The _____ eats corn.

6. Is the _____ lost?

My, My, What a Pie!

Circle the correct pizza.

1. Billy and Pedro get an equal share. How did they cut the pizza?

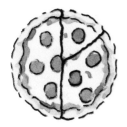   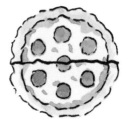

2. Dani, Josh, and Wen get an equal share. How did they cut the pizza?

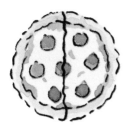   

3. Billy, Dani, Wen, and Josh get an equal share. How did they cut the pizza?

4. Circle the picture that shows $\frac{2}{3}$ of the apples colored.

Growing, Growing...

Josh grew a watermelon. In the spring, he planted seeds. He watered his plant each day. The sun made it grow. By summer, the watermelon was huge! He brought it to the fair. He won a blue ribbon!

Circle the answer.

1. Who is the story about?

     a. Dani   b. Josh   c. Pedro

2. What fruit was grown?

     a. apples   b. watermelon   c. bananas

3. What did the plant need?

     a. water, rain, clouds   b. soil, sun, plants   c. soil, water, sun

4. Write 1, 2, 3, 4 to show the order.

COOL FACT

In Arizona, the saguaro cactus can grow more than 60 feet tall!

Look at the front of each birdhouse. Write how many sides, corners, and square corners you can see for each.

1.

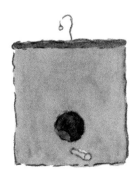

_____ sides

_____ corners

_____ square corners

2.

_____ sides

_____ corners

_____ square corners

3.

_____ sides

_____ corners

_____ square corners

4.

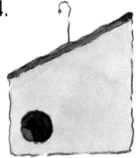

_____ sides

_____ corners

_____ square corners

5.

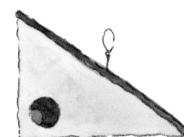

_____ sides

_____ corners

_____ square corners

6.

_____ sides

_____ corners

_____ square corners

GiGGLES

When you do not eat much, it is said you eat like me. But I am always eating, when I'm not nesting in a tree. Who am I?

A bird.

Cool Stuff for School

Summer is over. School will start soon.
The friends are doing some back-to-school shopping.

Use the grid on page 297 to see where each thing is
found. Write the aisle and row to find each item.
The first one is done for you.

1. Find the . Aisle __3__ Row __3__

2. Find the . Aisle _____ Row _____

3. Find the . Aisle _____ Row _____

4. Find the . Aisle _____ Row _____

5. Find the  . Aisle _____ Row _____

6. Find the . Aisle _____ Row _____

7. Find the . Aisle _____ Row _____

8. Find the . Aisle _____ Row _____

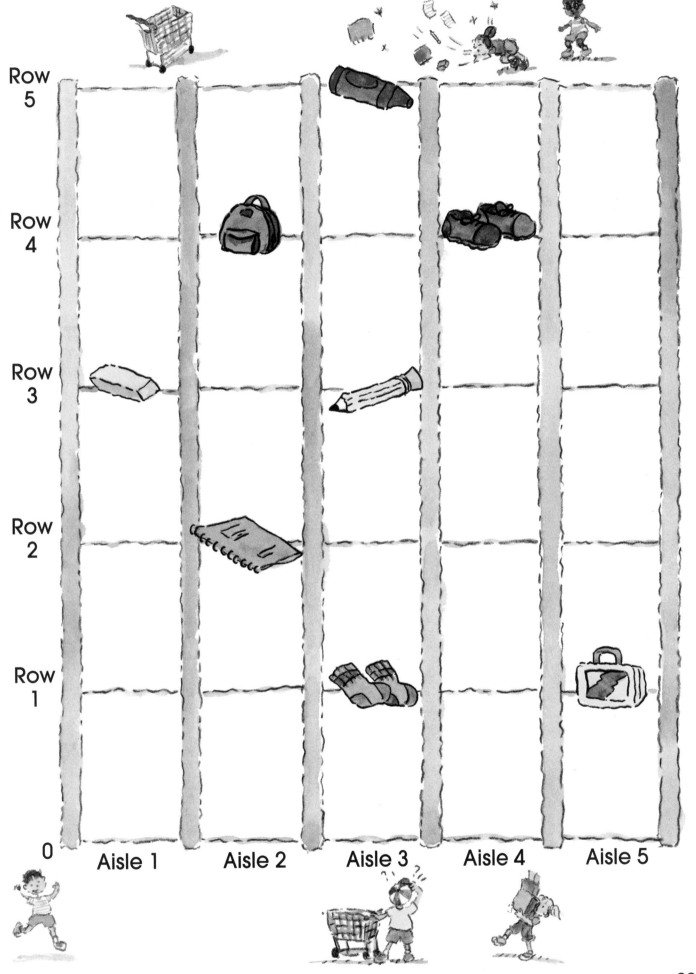

Row 5

Row 4

Row 3

Row 2

Row 1

0

Aisle 1   Aisle 2   Aisle 3   Aisle 4   Aisle 5

Back to School

Use <u>was</u> to tell about one.
Use <u>were</u> to tell about more than one.

Write in the correct verb to complete each sentence.

1. The friends _____ ready for school.

2. Dani _____ walking to school.

3. Pedro _____ waiting for Billy.

4. Wen and Josh _____ talking on the bus.

5. They _____ all happy to be back in school.

Next Summer

Use a period (.) to end a sentence that tells.
Use a (?) to end a sentence that asks.
Use this mark ⹀ to show where a capital letter goes.

Correct the sentences below by adding the proper marks.
The first one is done for you.

1. did you have a nice summer?
   ⹀

2. name one thing you did

3. will you take a trip next summer

4. do you know where you will go

5. i hope you have lots of fun

6. Write a sentence about what you did this summer.

Activities to Share

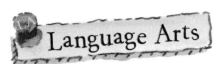

Here is a list of books with a summer theme, including books about the summer season, baseball, and travel. The list includes fiction and nonfiction selections for you to check out at your local library or bookstore. You can also find out about cool books and a summer reading club at **www.kidsreads.com**

Summer

- *52 Fun Things to Do at a Beach* by Lynn Gordon and illustrated by Karen Johnson. Chronicle Books, 1999. There are instructions for making sand dough, casting shadow monsters, sculpting portraits, and much more.

- *Crafts to Make in the Summer* by Kathy Ross and illustrated by Vicky Enright. Millbrook Press, 1999. Wonderful instructions and illustrations offer 29 easy-to-make craft projects with summertime themes, including a sunglasses case, a seashell candle holder, and a firecracker finger puppet.

- *How Do You Know It's Summer?* (Rookie Read About Science) by Allan Fowler. Children's Press, 1992. Children will recognize the typical signs of summer presented in this book, such as heat, thunderstorms, playtime, growing, and outdoor fun.

- *The Kids Summer Games Book* by Jane Drake and Ann Love and illustrated by Heather Collins. Kids Can Press, 1998. Your child will find hundreds of fun things to do in this book, including games to play with friends, alone, on the beach, or in the water, as well as activities to do outside in the sun and indoors on rainy days.

Baseball

- *Albert's Ballgame* by Leslie Tryon. Atheneum Press, 1996. This story is not about your ordinary baseball team. There are geese ballplayers instead of children!

- *Bats About Baseball* by Jean Little and Claire MacKay and illustrated by Kim Lafave. Viking, 1995. Ryder's grandmother goes nuts over baseball.

- *Playing Right Field* by Willy Welch and illustrated by Marc Simont. Scholastic, 1995. A boy daydreams about making a great play way out in right field.

Baseball fever got you? Slide into this Web site to find information about Little League: **www.littleleague.org**

Travel

When your family is on the road, you might want to check out these titles to provide your children with lots of things to do along the way!

- *Travel the Great States* by Sara jo Schwartz and illustrated by Terry Sirrell. School Zone Publishing, 1998.

- *52 Fun Things to Do in the Car* by Lynn Gordon and illustrated by Susan Synarski. Chronicle Books, 1994, and *52 Fun Things to Do on the Plane* by Lynn Gordon. Chronicle Books, 1996. The books deliver just as their titles suggest—lots of fun things to keep the little traveler busy!

- *Are We Almost There? The Kids' Book of Travel Fun* by Annette Laplaca and illustrated by Debbie Bryer. Harold Shaw Publishers, 1992. Another great book filled with activities to occupy travel time.

Not just books! Check out these videos and CD-ROMs.

Videos

Casey at the Bat
(CBS/Fox/Playhouse Video)
It's 1888 and Casey Frank saves Mudville's stadium and starts traditions we still see at baseball games today.

Let's Go Camping
(Vermont Storyworks 1-800-206-8383)
Ranger Ben offers information to take a fun and safe camping trip.

CD-ROMs

A Day at the Beach with the Fuzzooly Family
(Davidson CD-ROM)
Help the fuzzy character build a sandcastle, recycle litter, scuba dive, and learn safety tips.

Flash Action Software
(School Zone Interactive CD-ROM Series)
Review and practice skills throughout the summer. Titles include Numbers 1–100, Addition/Subtraction, and Alphabet.

Social Studies

- **A Day at the Beach**

Cool breezes, the smell of fresh salt air, the feel of sand between your toes—it's all at the beach! If you are planning a trip to the beach, here are a few tips for your family.

What to Bring: Make a list of things to bring, including sunscreen, sunglasses, towels, hats, pails, things to dig with, big T-shirts to wear for exploring, a sweatshirt if the air turns cool once the sun goes down, mesh bags for shell collecting, and a sieve or net to look at sea creatures up close for a short time.

To make great sandcastles, contact the experts at **www.unlitter.com**

Science

- *Nature All Year Long* by Clare Walker Leslie. Greenwillow, 1991.

Your child will learn about a variety of animals and their habitats during each season of the year. Details in scenes are numbered and labeled for easy identification. Suggestions for nature activities are included.

- *A Kid's Summer EcoJournal: With Nature Activities for Exploring the Season* by Toni Albert. Trickle Creek Books, 1998.

This book will encourage your child to explore, read, and write about nature. Activities include making a map, growing a flower, harvesting seeds, baking a potato with solar heat, collecting fireflies, following snails, and more.

- **High Tide, Low Tide**

If you and your family like to look for treasures on the beach, the best beachcombing happens right after the tide goes out during low tide. This is when you are likely to find treasures the high tide left behind. Look on the weather page of your local newspaper for the time of the tides.

- **A Seashore Zoo**

It's okay to collect sea creatures to observe as long as you return them to their habitat. First, make a habitat for them such as a pail or see-through container into which you have put sand, rocks, seaweed, and a container of seawater. Observe your sea creature for a while and then return it to the sand and sea. Draw a picture and write notes about what you observe.

- **Shell Wind Chimes**

Have you collected lots of shells from the beach? Make a wind chime by stringing some of the shells on a piece of driftwood. Thread string through a tiny hole in the shell and tie the length of string to the driftwood. Suspend five or more shells side by side. Hang it on your porch when you return home.

Here are a few cool Web sites to check out:
For a close-up look at sea animals, visit **www.seaworld.com**
For lots of fishy fun, visit **www.tetra-fish.com**

Math

- **Rainbow Snack**

Measure and mix these ingredients for a tasty anytime snack.

1 cup of colored fruit-flavored puffed cereal

1 cup of fruit-flavored cereal shaped like Os

1/2 cup sunflower seeds

1/2 cup peanuts or mixed nuts

1/2 cup raisins and other dried fruits

Place all the ingredients in a small plastic bag. Give it a good shake. Your snack is ready for travel!

Activities to Share

Helping Hand

Show your child how to set the table, dust the furniture, or some other task. Explain to your child that he or she has an important role in the family. Remember to praise your child for a job well done.

Autograph, Please!

Encourage your child to write fancy versions of his or her name. Add faces, legs, stripes, squiggles, or more. Cut out the name and its art and use it as a label for your child's lunch bag or room.

Read the Signs

Have your child read road signs and names of businesses as you travel in your car or on a bus. At the grocery store, encourage your child to read the signs to figure out which foods are found in each aisle.

Tic Tac Toe

Draw a tic-tac-toe board with three rows of three squares. In each square, draw a road sign, such as yield or no parking. When your child is traveling, encourage him or her to look for signs and cross them off as they are spotted.

Cooking Up Math

Take math into the kitchen where you and your child can follow a recipe, measure ingredients, and set timers. If your child has a favorite meal or snack, encourage him or her to write the recipe on a 3" by 5" card. Practice adding by making a double batch of the recipe. Explain to your child that each ingredient must be doubled.

Activities to Share

Story Problems

Challenge your child to solve addition and subtraction story problems throughout your day. For example, when you set the table, tell how many plates you are holding. Then place a few of the plates on the table. Ask your child how many you are holding now. At the playground, invent story problems based on children arriving at and leaving the swing set, the slide, or the sandbox. Encourage your child to make up story problems, too.

I Spy

Look for shapes and take turns guessing what the other person sees. For instance, find something square in the room. Have your child guess what it is. Ask your child to find an object that is another shape, and you must guess what he or she sees.

Word Collection

Give your child a box that will hold 3" by 5" cards. Each day have your child choose a word to learn. Write the word on a card and give it to your child. Your child may want to decorate the word card before storing it in the word box. Encourage your child to take the cards out of the box and read them. Help your child with any word that he or she has forgotten. Children need lots of practice to recognize words.

Where Did It Come From?

Help your child distinguish between natural and manufactured objects. Point out an object, such as a building, a tree, or a paper clip, and ask your child, "Where did it come from?" Your child must answer nature or people.

Make a Book

Staple sheets of blank paper together. Ask your child to make up a story. Have your child tell who the story is about and what will happen to that character. Decide whether you or your child will write the words of the story in the book. Encourage your child to illustrate the story. Read the story to your child and have your child read the story to you.

Answers

Page 2

Fun Stuff
mouse house
fat cat
goat boat

Page 3

1. 3+3=6
2. 6-3=3
3. 4+3=7
4. 5+2=7
5. 7-5=2

Page 6

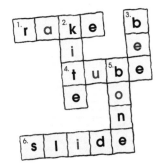

Page 7

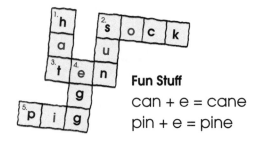

Fun Stuff
can + e = cane
pin + e = pine

Page 8

1. 4:00   2. 9:30
3. 8:30   4. 2:00

5:00 Cowboy Sam
5:30 Dinosaurs!
7:00 Joke Time
7:30 Camp Talk

Page 4

1. square
2. triangle
3. rectangle
4. triangle
5. rectangle

Page 5

Page 9

Page 10

1. true
2. true
3. false
4. true
5. false
6. true

Page 11

1. Do you like dinosaurs?
2. Two dinosaurs are running.
3. Can some dinosaurs swim?
4. The big dinosaur is green.
5. Some dinosaurs eat plants.
6. How many spots does the small dinosaur have?

Pages 12–13

Estimates will vary.
1. 3 in.
2. 1 in.
3. 4 in.
4. 2 in.
5. 4 cm
6. 6.5 cm
7. 11.5 cm
8. 9 cm

Page 14

4 have animals have fur.
3 have feathers.

Page 15

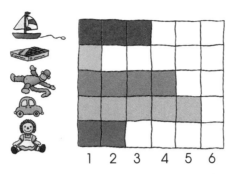

4 animals have 4 legs.
2 animals have 2 legs.
2 animals have 6 legs.
1 animal has no legs.

Page 16

Page 17

Page 18

1. dogs
2. cats
3. tails
4. bones
5. pals

Page 19

1. Polly
2. Puff
3. Peter
4. Bubbles
5. Duke

Fun Stuff
Circle the words **cats**,
frogs, **dogs**, and **dogs**.

Page 20

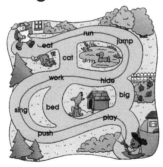

Page 21

1. $3+4=7$

2. $4+2=6$

3. $6-2=4$

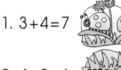

Pages 22–23

1. 12
2. January
3. August
4. winter
5. spring
6. Month will vary.

Page 24

Page 25

	E	5
	F	1
	H	4

	B	5
	C	3
	H	2

Page 26

1. hot
2. eat
3. cave
4. hands
5. little
6. hear

Fun Stuff
Both have wings.
Both can jump.

Page 30

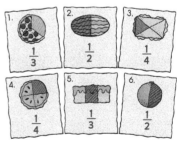

Cool Idea

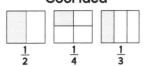

Page 27

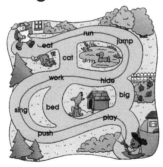

Page 28

1. longer
2. longest
3. fastest
4. fast
5. faster

Page 29

1. near a wall
2. 10 steps away
3. penny
4. into a hole
Circle 10 pennies.

Answers

Page 31

hat   cat   bat
fan   van   pan
had   mad   sad
man   ran   can

Page 32

cat
sat   pat   mat
nap   tap   cap

Page 33

Page 34

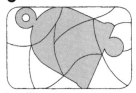

bell
get   wet   pet
ten   pen   hen

Page 35

Page 36

1. big
2. give
3. his
4. fish
5. pig
6. six

Page 37

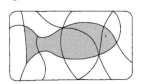

fish
wig   dig
dish   wish

Page 38

fox   doll
hot   not   lot
box

Page 39

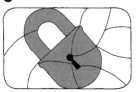

lock
dot   got   not
fox   box

Page 40

Page 41

sun   bug
rug   cup
hug   bus

Page 42

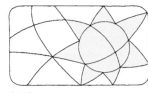

sun
rug   hug   bug
hut   cut   nut

Page 43

short a
short e
short i
short o
short u

Page 44

Long a   Long i
rake   **kite**

Long o   Long u
home   **tube**
Drawings should resemble
the written words.

Page 45

```
                              K
        B O N E              I
    P       I   O            T
    L       K   T U B E      E
    C A K E     E
    N
M U L E
```

Page 46

1. snail
2. rain
3. train
4. tail

    pail   paint

Page 47

1. play
2. day
3. stay

    say   hay   may

Page 48

Page 49

meet   feet
she   be
seal   leaf

team   meat

Page 50

1. seal
2. tree
3. leaf
4. bee

    me   he

Page 51

cry   find
fly   mind

night   nine
right   vine

light   tight

Page 52

fish	find	book
out	fly	his
kid	right	you

pick	pig	night
six	cry	make
mind	this	bat

sky	car	home
not	tight	with
will	see	kind

Page 53

1. boat
2. coat
3. toad
4. goat

    no   so   go

Page 54

snow   slow   grow
cold   told   sold

crow, gold

Page 55

grow	ring	wake	dog	bell
cold	toad	plum	sled	band
tack	snow	go	goat	took
book	wall	sing	sold	slow
pet	time	bird	chair	told

Page 56

new   flew

zoo   soon
school

blue

Page 57

1. zoo	blew	run	snow
2. blue	boy	food	cup
3. new	find	cry	moon
4. soon	dew	rose	rain
5. school	cold	glue	box
6. flew	nest	low	tool

Page 58

Page 59

1. clean   2. night
3. cold   4. sleep
5. sweet   6. me
7. go   8. take
9. white   10. dry
11. over   12. low

Page 60

Answers

Page 93
1. 3 + 2 = 5
2. 1 + 1 = 2
3. 4 + 2 = 6

Page 94
1. 3 + 3 = 6
2. 4 + 2 = 6
3. 5 + 1 = 6

Page 95
1. 3 + 4 = 7
2. 5 + 2 = 7
3. 3 + 5 = 8

Page 96
1. 7
2. 6
3. 8
4. 8

Page 97

1. 7 birds,   2
            + 5
            ―――
              7

2. 8 dogs,   3
            + 5
            ―――
              8

3. 8 kittens, 2
             + 6
             ―――
               8

Page 98

1. 9 books,   4
            + 5
            ―――
              9

2. 9 pens,   3
            + 6
            ―――
              9

3. 10 stamps, 5
             + 5
             ―――
               10

Page 99
1. 4, 2, 2
2. 5, 3, 2
3. 6, 4, 2

Page 100
1. 6, 6 – 1 = 5
2. 6, 6 – 4 = 2
3. 5, 5 – 3 = 2

Page 101
1. 3   2. 2
3. 4   4. 4
5. 2   6. 3

Page 102
1. 8 – 3 = 5, 5
2. 7 – 2 = 5, 5
3. 8 – 6 = 2, 2
4. 7 – 5 = 2, 2

Page 103

1. 2 bees,   5
            – 3
            ―――
              2

2. 2 bears,   6
            – 4
            ―――
              2

3. 4 jars,   6
            – 2
            ―――
              4

Page 104

1. 4 birds,   8
            – 4
            ―――
              4

2. 4 apples, 6
            – 2
            ―――
              4

3. 5 shells, 8
            – 3
            ―――
              5

Page 105

1. 6 apples,   8
             – 2
             ―――
               6

2. 9 pears,   5
             + 4
             ―――
               9

3. 3 bananas, 7
             – 4
             ―――
               3

Page 106

1.   6
    – 2
    ―――
      4

2.   7
    – 3
    ―――
      4

3.   9
    – 4
    ―――
      5

4.   8
    – 4
    ―――
      4

Page 107
1. 4
2. 5
3. 3
4. 2
5. 6
6. 5
7. 3 + 5 = 8
8. 6 – 4 = 2

Page 108
1. 5
2. 3
3. 2
4. 7
5. 2 + 4 = 6
6. 7 – 5 = 2

Page 109
1. 6
2. 4
3. 4 + 2 = 6
4. 8 + 2 = 10
5. 8 – 4 = 4
6. 4 + 6 = 10

Page 110
1. 6
2. 10
3. 8
4. 8 − 6 = 2
5. 10 − 6 = 4
6. 6 + 8 = 14

Page 111
1. 7 cherries, $\begin{array}{r} 9 \\ -2 \\ \hline 7 \end{array}$
2. 11 worms, $\begin{array}{r} 7 \\ +4 \\ \hline 11 \end{array}$
3. 12 squirrels, $\begin{array}{r} 6 \\ +6 \\ \hline 12 \end{array}$

Page 112
1. 5 pennies, $\begin{array}{r} 9 \\ -4 \\ \hline 5 \end{array}$
2. 13 nickels, $\begin{array}{r} 4 \\ 3 \\ +6 \\ \hline 13 \end{array}$
3. 6 dimes, $\begin{array}{r} 9 \\ -3 \\ \hline 6 \end{array}$

Page 113
1. 7 presents, $\begin{array}{r} 11 \\ -4 \\ \hline 7 \end{array}$
2. 3 balloons, $\begin{array}{r} 10 \\ -7 \\ \hline 3 \end{array}$
3. 15 cupcakes, $\begin{array}{r} 11 \\ +4 \\ \hline 15 \end{array}$

Page 114
1. $\begin{array}{r} 10 \\ -5 \\ \hline 5 \end{array}$
2. $\begin{array}{r} 11 \\ +3 \\ \hline 14 \end{array}$
3. $\begin{array}{r} 8 \\ +7 \\ \hline 15 \end{array}$
4. $\begin{array}{r} 12 \\ -3 \\ \hline 9 \end{array}$

Page 115
1. 12 hens, $\begin{array}{r} 7 \\ +5 \\ \hline 12 \end{array}$
2. 13 chicks, $\begin{array}{r} 8 \\ +5 \\ \hline 13 \end{array}$
3. 8 eggs, $\begin{array}{r} 12 \\ -4 \\ \hline 8 \end{array}$

Page 116
1. 7 postcards, $\begin{array}{r} 14 \\ -7 \\ \hline 7 \end{array}$
2. 19 sailboats, $\begin{array}{r} 13 \\ +6 \\ \hline 19 \end{array}$
3. 7 fish, $\begin{array}{r} 15 \\ -8 \\ \hline 7 \end{array}$

Page 117
1. 12 fishhooks, $\begin{array}{r} 16 \\ -4 \\ \hline 12 \end{array}$
2. 18 pictures, $\begin{array}{r} 13 \\ +5 \\ \hline 18 \end{array}$
3. 5 shells, $\begin{array}{r} 12 \\ -7 \\ \hline 5 \end{array}$

Page 118
1. 24 tulips, $\begin{array}{r} 13 \\ +11 \\ \hline 24 \end{array}$
2. 37 plants, $\begin{array}{r} 23 \\ +14 \\ \hline 37 \end{array}$
3. 21 butterflies, $\begin{array}{r} 34 \\ -13 \\ \hline 21 \end{array}$
4. 10¢, $\begin{array}{r} 25¢ \\ -15¢ \\ \hline 10¢ \end{array}$

Page 119
1. $\begin{array}{r} 8¢ \\ +4¢ \\ \hline 12¢ \end{array}$
2. $\begin{array}{r} 3¢ \\ 4¢ \\ +5¢ \\ \hline 12¢ \end{array}$
3. $\begin{array}{r} 14¢ \\ -6¢ \\ \hline 8¢ \end{array}$
4. $\begin{array}{r} 17¢ \\ -4¢ \\ \hline 13¢ \end{array}$

Page 120
1. $\begin{array}{r} 48¢ \\ -6¢ \\ \hline 42¢ \end{array}$
2. $\begin{array}{r} 11¢ \\ +8¢ \\ \hline 19¢ \end{array}$
3. $\begin{array}{r} 7¢ \\ +9¢ \\ \hline 16¢ \end{array}$
4. $\begin{array}{r} 15¢ \\ -3¢ \\ \hline 12¢ \end{array}$
5. $\begin{array}{r} 6¢ \\ +5¢ \\ \hline 11¢ \end{array}$
6. $\begin{array}{r} 12¢ \\ -7¢ \\ \hline 5¢ \end{array}$

Page 121
1. $\begin{array}{r} 43 \\ -37 \\ \hline 6 \end{array}$
2. $\begin{array}{r} 29 \\ +34 \\ \hline 63 \end{array}$
3. $\begin{array}{r} 58 \\ +18 \\ \hline 76 \end{array}$
4. $\begin{array}{r} 56 \\ -38 \\ \hline 18 \end{array}$

Page 122
1. $\begin{array}{r} 148 \\ -129 \\ \hline 19 \end{array}$
2. $\begin{array}{r} 138 \\ +126 \\ \hline 264 \end{array}$
3. $\begin{array}{r} 87 \\ -79 \\ \hline 8 \end{array}$
4. $\begin{array}{r} 116 \\ +118 \\ \hline 234 \end{array}$

Answers

Page 123
1. 7¢
2. 20¢
3. 30¢
4. 13¢

Page 124
1. 10 20 30 40 50 51 52-**52¢**
2. 10 20 30 35 40 41-**41¢**
3. 10 15 20 21 22 23-**23¢**
4. 10 20 25 30 31-**31¢**

Page 125
1. 10¢
2. 33¢
3. 18¢
4. 25¢
5. 27¢
6. 36¢

Page 126
1. 25¢
2. 25¢
3. (28¢)
4. 25¢

Page 127
1. 36¢
2. 55¢
3. 76¢
4. 52¢
5. 87¢

Page 128
1. 25 35 45 50 51¢ Yes
2. 25 50 60 65¢ No
3. 10 20 25 30¢ Yes
4. 25 50 75 76¢ Yes
5. 10 20 30 31 32¢ No

Page 129
Answers can vary.

	Half Dollar	Quarter	Dime	Nickel	Penny
53¢	1				3
27¢		1			2
18¢			1	1	3
50¢	1				
68¢	1		1	1	3
34¢		1		1	4
76¢	1	1			1
15¢			1	1	
37¢		1	1		2
72¢	1		2		2

Page 130
1. 48¢
2. (50¢)
3. (50¢)
4. 60¢
5. 39¢
6. (50¢)

Page 131
1. 39¢ + 28¢ = 67¢
2. 44¢ + 45¢ = 89¢
3. 44¢ + 17¢ = 61¢
4. 36¢ + 39¢ = 75¢
5. 36¢ + 45¢ = 81¢
6. 17¢ + 28¢ = 45¢

Page 132

Across	Down
a. 60	a. 62
b. 42	b. 45
c. 95	c. 90
d. 30	d. 35
e. 25	e. 25
f. 15	f. 10
g. 100	g. 10
h. 50	h. 55
i. 75	i. 74
j. 84	j. 89

Page 133

Page 134

Page 135

Page 136

Page 137
1. 1/**2**
2. 1/**3**
3. 1/**4**
4. 1/**2**
5. 1/**3**
6. 1/**4**

Page 138
1. **2**/4
2. **3**/4
3. **1**/2
4. **4**/6
5. **1**/4
6. **1**/3

Page 139
1. 1/2
2. 1/4
3. 1/3
4. 1/4
5. 1/3
6. 1/4
7. 1/3
8. 1/3
9. 1/4

Page 140
1. 3/4
2. 1/3
3. 3/8
4. 1/4
5. 2/6
6. 1/3
7. 2/3
8. 2/4
9. 1/2

Page 141
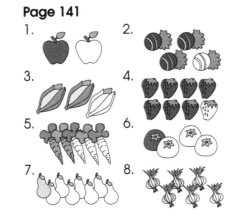

Page 142
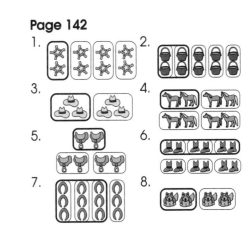

Page 143

Page 144
1. 2 o'clock
   2:00
2. 7 o'clock
   7:00
3. 9 o'clock
   9:00
4. 11 o'clock
   11:00
5. 8 o'clock
   8:00
6. 5 o'clock
   5:00

Page 145
1. Half past 4
   4:30
2. Half past 10
   10:30
3. Half past 6
   6:30
4. Half past 8
   8:30
5. Half past 12
   12:30
6. Half past 3
   3:30

Page 146
1. 1:30
2. 6:00
3. 9:30
4. 10:30
5. 12:00
6. 5:30

Page 147
Answers are clockwise.

5, 10, 15, 20, 25, 30, 35, 40, 45, 50, 55, 60
60 minutes

Page 148
1. Quarter past 6
   6:15
2. Quarter past 8
   8:15
3. Quarter past 1
   1:15
4. Quarter past 12
   12:15
5. Quarter past 10
   10:15
6. Quarter past 7
   7:15

Page 149
1. Quarter to 4
   3:45
2. Quarter to 9
   8:45
3. Quarter to 1
   12:45
4. Quarter to 7
   6:45
5. Quarter to 2
   1:45
6. Quarter to 10
   9:45

Page 150
1. 1:45
2. 2:15
3. 7:45
4. 11:15
5. 3:45
6. 8:15

Page 151
1. 4:05
2. 5:15
3. 3:10
4. 6:35
5. 9:50
6. 2:20

Page 152
1. 9:15
2. 6:00
3. 5:20
4. 10:45
5. 4:40
6. 11:30

Answers

Page 153

3, 6
2, 3
5, 1
7, 8

Page 154

0, 1
2, 3, 4
5, 6, 7, 8
9, 10, 11, 12

Page 155

1. 5, 7
2. 8, 3

Page 156

1. 5 bears, 5 owls
2. 7 puffins, 8 whales
3. 3 musk oxen, 12 wolves

 4

Page 157

1. 4 beavers, 2 dragonflies
2. 3 bats, 1 raccoon
3. 6 owls, 5 lightning bugs

 9

Page 158

1	2	3	4	5	6	7	8	9	10
11	12	13	14	15	16	17	18	19	20
21	22	23	24	25	26	27	28	29	30
31	32	33	34	35	36	37	38	39	40
41	42	43	44	45	46	47	48	49	50
51	52	53	54	55	56	57	58	59	60
61	62	63	64	65	66	67	68	69	70
71	72	73	74	75	76	77	78	79	80
81	82	83	84	85	86	87	88	89	90
91	92	93	94	95	96	97	98	99	100

Page 159

1 2 **3** 4 5 **6** 7 **8 9** 10
41 **42 43 44** 45 46 **47** 48 **49** 50
71 72 73 **74** 75 **76 77** 78 **79 80**
31 **32 33 34** 35 **36** 37 **38 39 40**
81 82 83 **84 85 86 87** 88 **89** 90
61 **62 63 64 65 66 67 68 69** 70

Page 160

1. 1 + 1 = 2   1 + 2 = 3
2. 1 + 3 = 4   1 + 4 = 5
3. 2 + 1 = 3   2 + 2 = 4
4. 2 + 3 = 5   4 + 1 = 5

Page 161

1.
$$\begin{array}{r} 2 \\ +1 \\ \hline 3 \end{array} \quad \begin{array}{r} 1 \\ +4 \\ \hline 5 \end{array}$$

3.
$$\begin{array}{r} 2 \\ +3 \\ \hline 5 \end{array} \quad \begin{array}{r} 1 \\ +1 \\ \hline 2 \end{array}$$

2.
$$\begin{array}{r} 3 \\ +2 \\ \hline 5 \end{array} \quad \begin{array}{r} 1 \\ +3 \\ \hline 4 \end{array}$$

4.
$$\begin{array}{r} 2 \\ +2 \\ \hline 4 \end{array} \quad \begin{array}{r} 3 \\ +2 \\ \hline 5 \end{array}$$

Page 162

Brown 3
Red 1
Yellow 2
Green 4
Blue 6
Black 5

Page 163

1. 3 − 1 = 2   4 − 1 = 3
2. 6 − 2 = 4   5 − 2 = 3
3. 6 − 3 = 3   5 − 1 = 4
4. 7 − 2 = 5   7 − 3 = 4

Page 164

1.
$$\begin{array}{r} 5 \\ -1 \\ \hline 4 \end{array} \quad \begin{array}{r} 7 \\ -2 \\ \hline 5 \end{array}$$

2.
$$\begin{array}{r} 7 \\ -3 \\ \hline 4 \end{array} \quad \begin{array}{r} 4 \\ -1 \\ \hline 3 \end{array}$$

3.
$$\begin{array}{r} 5 \\ -2 \\ \hline 3 \end{array} \quad \begin{array}{r} 8 \\ -3 \\ \hline 5 \end{array}$$

4.
$$\begin{array}{r} 6 \\ -2 \\ \hline 4 \end{array} \quad \begin{array}{r} 3 \\ -1 \\ \hline 2 \end{array}$$

Page 165

Page 166

+	0	1	2	3	4	5
0	0	1	2	3	4	5
1	1	2	3	4	5	
2	2	3	4	5		
3	3	4	5			
4	4	5				
5	5					

Page 167

1. 7, 9, 8, 8
2. 12, 7, 9, 11
3. 8, 11, 10, 12

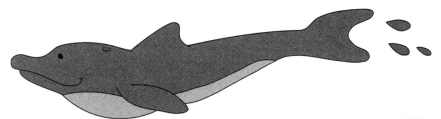

Page 168

1. 7
   5
   8
   10
2. 7
   4
   10
   8
3. 6
   9
   5
   12
4. 9
   12
   8
   5

Page 169

1. 8, 2
2. 6, 3
3. 7, 5
4. 7, 4

Page 170

1. 3, 6, 4
2. 3, 5, 8
3. 5, 9, 5
4. 7, 7, 4

Page 171

| 3 | +2 | 5 | -2 | 3 | +4 | 7 | +3 | 10 |

Page 172

10, **20**, 30, **40**, **50**
60, 70, **80**, **90**, **100**

Page 173

1. 2, 5   2, 6
   25   26
2. 3, 8   3, 4
   38   34
3. 2, 8   2, 9
   28   29

Page 174

1. 5, 6, 56
2. 3, 2, 32
3. 4, 7, 47
4. 6, 8, 68

Page 175

1. tens ones
   2   5
   4   3
   2   8
   3   0
   5   4
   6   5

2. tens ones
   1   7
   7   1
   6   6
   1   9
   8   1
   4   0

Page 176

1. 26, 45
2. 41, 53
3. 70, 19
4. 25, 64
5. 8, 92
6. 86, 50
7. 37, 22

Page 177

Before
1. 17, 32
2. 23, 66
3. 80, 29
4. 44, 26

After
5. 23, 12
6. 19, 38
7. 28, 7
8. 39, 70

Page 178

Greater
1. 23, 50, 31
2. 21, 35, 15
3. 18, 31, 43

Less
4. 48, 25, 23
5. 59, 13, 25
6. 58, 44, 78

Page 179

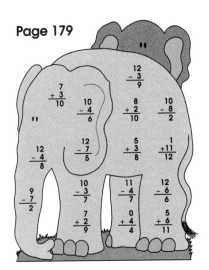

Page 180

1. 9, 5, 12, 6
2. 12, 8, 10, 12
3. 4, 8, 6, 9
4. 5, 11, 5, 8

Page 181

1. Answers given
2. 6 - 1, 5 + 0, 9 - 4
3. 10 - 2, 4 + 4, 2 + 6
4. 6 + 4, 7 + 3, 11 - 1
5. 12 - 0, 8 + 4, 7 + 5
6. 3 + 3, 12 - 6, 5 + 1
7. 9 + 2, 5 + 6, 8 + 3
8. 7 + 0, 11 - 4, 4 + 3

Page 182

Answers

Pages 184–185
Bank, Firehouse, Grocery, Hospital, Post Office, School, Toy Shop, Zippity Zoo

Pages 186–187

4. Answers will vary.
5. yes
6. yes
7. no

Page 183

1. swan 2. bobcat 3. zebra

Page 188

Page 189
fast, stop, top, pat, ten, tent, tub, bat at, trap, rap, pot; *counterclockwise*: fat, top, par, part, tab, but, net, tap, pot, pots

Page 190
number words: five, one, four, four, one, three, three, one, two, two, one, one, one
words that rhyme with tip: 1. dip 2. slip 3. trip 4. flip; other words: chip, clip, drip, hip, grip, lip, nip, rip, ship, sip, skip, snip, yip, zip

Page 191

1. 3   2. 6
3. 3 or 8   4. 2
5. 4   6. 1

Page 192

1. snake   2. swan
3. spider   4. skunk
5. slug   6. starfish

```
x  b  s  k  u  n  k
v  s  t  o  p  s  g
s  w  a  n  g  n  s
f  t  r  y  c  o  l
t  u  f  z  j  w  u
s  p  i  d  e  r  g
y  o  s  n  a  k  e
p  q  h  s  n  a  p
```

Page 193
missing numerals: 4, 3, 6, 5, 6, 9, 6, 10, 8, 11, 6

Page 194
1. under 2. on 3. over
4. across 5. in

Page 195
Circle Jan, Bob, Chan, and Lisa.
1. Bob 2. Jan 3. Lisa 4. Chan

Page 196
1. Jungle World
2. Quackers Pond
3. Zebra Park
4. Monkey Island
Bear Cave

Page 197
4 + 3 = 7 tigers
6 + 3 = 9 leopards
4 + 2 = 6 bobcats
5 + 4 = 9 lions

Pages 198–199
1. Names will vary.   2. 1 + 2 = 3
3. 3 - 1 = 2   4. 2 + 3 = 5
5. 5 - 2 = 3   6. 3 + 3 = 6
7. 6 - 2 = 4   8. 4 - 4 = 0

Page 200
1. slide
2. jump
3. dig
4. climb

Page 201

1. pup   2. cub

Pages 202–203
1. robin
2. fish
3. snake
4. chick

Page 206
1. 6 + 4 = 10   2. 5 - 4 = 1
3. 4 + 2 = 6   4. 5 - 3 = 2
5. 7 + 5 = 12   6. 5 - 2 = 3

Page 204

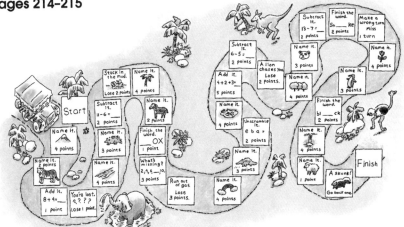

1. can't ———— Where is
2. Let's ———— can not
3. Where's ——— is not
4. isn't ———— Let us

Page 205
1. Tuesday   2. Thursday
3. Monday   4. Saturday

Page 207
1. wet   2. huge
3. tiny   4. sleepy
5. long   6. tall

Page 208
1. 14
2. 2

Page 209
glad: happy, sad
noisy: loud, quiet
little: small, big
quick: fast, slow

Page 210
Animal names will vary.
Stories will vary. Make sure that
stories have two characters that
solve a problem.

Page 211

	weight in pounds
tiger cub	
baby porcupine	
fox	
snowy owl	
fawn	
opossum	
weight in pounds	1 2 3 4 5 6 7 8 9 10

Page 212

Put In	Take Out	How Many Are Left?	Put In	Put In	How Many in All?
9	2	7	9	6	15
10	4	6	2	8	10
12	7	5	6	5	11
8	6	2	7	7	14
15	8	7	8	6	14

Page 213
1. Ben
2. Anna
3. Mom
4. Dad

Pages 214–215

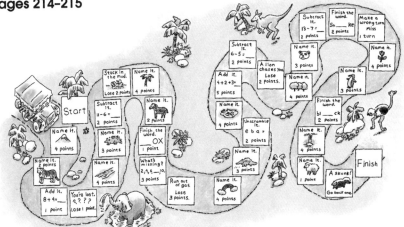

mountain; tiger; 12; river or stream; porcupine; 5; palm tree;
zebra; box or fox; 8; rainbow; anteater; bear or bare;
pond; 9; 1; trees or forest; panda; 6; snake; tulip
or flower; penguin; block or black; waterfall; sheep

Page 216

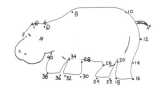

1. fat
2. water
3. grass
4. hippo

Page 217
1. to the water fountain
2. flag
3. parrot
4. 2, 1, 3

5.

Answers

Page 218

5	10	6	22	13	8
11	15	7	18	31	14
17	20	25	32	47	71
36	22	30	35	40	48
51	56	43	33	45	50

Page 219

4.

Page 220

Drawings will vary.

Page 221

Page 222

The Stars of the Show

1. o p o s s u m
2. d e e r
3. s k u n k
4. s q u i r r e l

Riddles will vary.

Page 223

6:00   9:30   7:00

5:30   8:00   7:30

Page 224

1. B
2. E
3. A
4. D
5. C

Page 225

Kinds of Animals		Animals We Want	Animals We Have	How Many More Do We Need?
camel		8	4	4
deer		15	9	6
giraffe		10	7	3
hippo		12	8	4
pig		14	7	7
sheep		18	9	9
buffalo		9	5	4
moose		13	6	7

Page 226

5 +8	12 -6	8 +2	5 +7	10 -3
13	6	10	12	7
-7	+3	-5	-6	+7
6	9	5	6	14
+4	+3	+7	+8	-6
10	12	12	14	8

moose

Page 227

Page 228

1. No
2. No
3. Yes
4. tracks
5. the forest
6. last night

Page 229

$\frac{1}{2}$

$\frac{1}{4}$

$\frac{1}{3}$

$\frac{2}{2}$

$\frac{3}{4}$

$\frac{2}{3}$

Page 230

2. 25¢ 25¢ 25¢ 10¢ 1¢; Yes
3. 25¢ 10¢ 10¢ 10¢ 10¢; Yes
4. 25¢ 10¢ 10¢ 5¢ 5¢; No

Page 231

1. 20¢
  + 75¢
  ——
  95¢

2. 44¢
  + 50¢
  ——
  94¢

3. 42¢
  + 34¢
  ——
  76¢

4. 35¢
  + 52¢
  ——
  87¢

Page 232

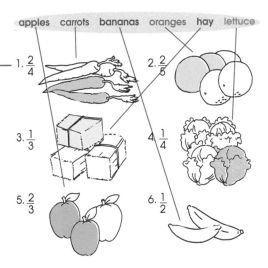

apples carrots bananas oranges hay lettuce

1. $\frac{2}{4}$ 2. $\frac{2}{5}$ 3. $\frac{1}{3}$ 4. $\frac{1}{4}$ 5. $\frac{2}{3}$ 6. $\frac{1}{2}$

Page 233

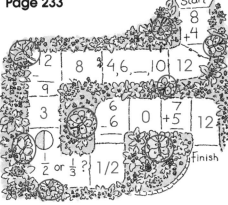

8 butterflies

Page 234

Letters will vary but should follow correct letter form.

Page 235

Guesses will vary.

Pages 236–237

1. long tails
2. short tails
3. Bears' tails changed because Bear froze his tail in the pond and broke it off when he pulled it out of the ice.

Page 238

Reasons children like zoos will vary.

Answers

Page 242

```
S  T  W  E  N  W
B  I  L  L  Y  T
L  P  E  D  R  O
K  C  D  A  N  I
G  J  O  S  H  J
```

Page 243

swim
camp
fish
ride
hike
baseball
Answer will vary.

Page 244

Summer things:

beach towel
shorts
picnic
beach ball

baseball cap
suitcase
swimsuit
watermelon

Page 245

Names by houses in clockwise order:

Pedro

Billy

Wen

Page 246

Page 247

1. Pedro
2. Billy
3. Wen
4. Dani
5. Josh

Page 248

6 innings
Rockets

Page 249

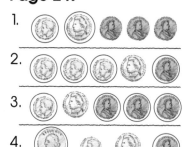

1.
2.
3.
4.

Page 250

4 Slippery Slide
3 Paddleboats
6 Wave Pool
2 Log Ride
5 Tube Trails
1 Beach
Answer will vary.

Page 251

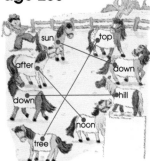

Page 252

1. in
2. cool
3. big
4. loud
5. fast
6. happy

Page 253

Answer will vary.

Pages 254-255

1. ghost town
2. no
3. yes

4. coyote
5. pond
Answer will vary.

Page 256

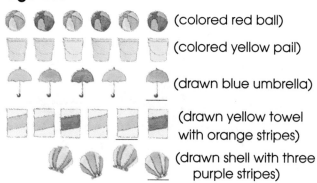

Page 257

Josh	Dani
50¢	50¢
30¢	20¢
10¢	15¢
2¢	1¢
92¢	86¢

Josh has saved more money.

Pages 258-259

1. Yes
2. Yes
3. No
4. No
5. Yes
6. Yes

Page 260

(colored red ball)

(colored yellow pail)

(drawn blue umbrella)

(drawn yellow towel with orange stripes)

(drawn shell with three purple stripes)

Page 261

Living Things:
crab
lifeguard
seagulls
shells (some shells are living)

Non-Living Things:
boat
flag
kite
shells

Page 262

Page 263

1. octopus
2. blowfish
3. hermit crab
4. sawfish
5. dolphin

Page 264

Coyote Desert
Black Bear Forest
Turtle Island
Giant Mountain

Page 265

1. cold
2. hot
3. dry
4. water
5. trees

Billy's family is going to Coyote Desert.

Page 266

1. bike
2. bus
3. car
4. jet
5. train

Page 267

Art and answers will vary.
Look at the images to review art

Pages 268-269

Postcard names from left to right:
Pedro, Dani and Josh, Billy, Wen

1. bear
2. ocean
3. calf
4. horse
5. desert

Page 270

Number of fish:
6, 10, 6, 4, 8

Page 271

Length of fish
(by pennies)
2
6
2
4
3
Estimations will vary but should be relatively close.

Page 272

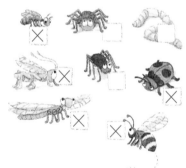

Page 273

There are 13 insects.
Insect drawings will vary.

Page 274

They washed 4 dogs.

Page 275

1. Thursday
2. Sunday
3. Wednesday
4. Saturday

Page 276

1. 7
   Because it rained.
2. 10
   Because it was sunny.
3. Cloudy days
Bonus: July

Page 277

1. 11
2. 8
3. 12
4. 6
5. 9
6. 5

Page 278

1. apples - 6
2. bananas - 7
3. carrots - 8
4. lettuce - 4
5. melons - 3
6. potatoes - 5

Page 279

1. apples
2. lettuce
3. bananas
4. apples
Check child's graph. Shaded areas should match the numbers found on page 278.

Page 280

1. 3 tens 2 ones 32
2. 4 tens 0 ones 40
3. 3 tens 4 ones 34
4. 5 tens 3 ones 53
5. 3 tens 0 ones 30
6. 3 tens 6 ones 36

	tens	ones
40	4	0
36	3	6

Page 281

Pedro picked 50 berries.
Billy picked 100 berries.

Page 282

Page 283

1. parade
2. Pedro
3. Drums
4. Bells
5. town

Page 284

1. Wen
2. holiday
3. July 4
4. 2:00 P.M.
5. 123 Shady Lane
Answers will vary.

Page 285

1. brings milk
2. has bananas
3. takes a salad
4. carries hot dogs
5. eat together
Answers will vary.
Bonus Question: Pedro

Page 286

Let's watch!
Isn't this great?
Don't blink!
We're lucky!
I'm watching!

Page 287

1. 2:00
2. 10:00
3. 6:00
4. 11:00
5. 5:00

Pages 288-289 Totals include the participants.

1. 6 people
2. 8 people
3. the roping contest
4. the flower show

Page 290

1. 2:00 2:30
2. 5:00 5:30
3. 7:00 7:30

4. 8:00
5. 11:30

6. 3:00
7. 4:30

Page 291

	quarter	dime	nickel	penny
8¢	0	0	1	3
15¢	0	1	1	0
20¢	0	2	0	0
46¢	1	2	0	1
39¢	1	1	0	4
58¢	2	0	1	3

Other coin variations acceptable.

Page 292

1. horse
2. pig
3. goat
4. cow
5. duck
6. dog

Page 293

1.
2.
3.

4.

Page 294

1. b
2. b
3. c
4. 2, 1, 4, 3

Page 295

1. 4, 4, 4
2. 3, 3, 0
3. 4, 4, 4
4. 4, 4, 2
5. 3, 3, 1
6. 5, 5, 2

Pages 296-297

1. Aisle 3, Row 3
2. Aisle 2, Row 2
3. Aisle 5, Row 1
4. Aisle 2, Row 4
5. Aisle 1, Row 3
6. Aisle 3, Row 5
7. Aisle 3, Row 1
8. Aisle 4, Row 4

Page 298

1. were
2. was
3. was
4. were
5. were

Page 299

1. did you have a nice summer?
2. name one thing you did.
3. will you take a trip next summer?
4. do you know where you will go?
5. i hope you have lots of fun.
6. Answer will vary.

  Big First Grade Pencil Pal 08253